ENTHEOGENS
and
the FUTURE
of RELIGION

"This book provides a balanced, thoroughly researched, and clear account about a topic that has fascinated people for centuries—even millennia—and will be with us, one way or another, for a long time to come."

HARVEY COX, PH.D., PROFESSOR OF DIVINITY AT HARVARD
UNIVERSITY AND AUTHOR OF *THE FUTURE OF FAITH*

"This book of essays plows new ground in the relationship between entheogens and religion. It is well worth reading. Any path that can bring the human family closer together should be investigated."

REV. DR. KENNETH B. SMITH, PRESIDENT OF
THE CHICAGO THEOLOGY SEMINARY

"An important book for anyone who cares about the future of the human race. The sensible use of entheogens is one of most promising paths to deep spiritual insight for many people, and this book shows how that could be done—if we care enough."

CHARLES T. TART, PH.D., PROFESSOR EMERITUS OF
PSYCHOLOGY, UNIVERSITY OF CALIFORNIA

"We have long needed this well-articulated, thoughtful, and rational basis for understanding the power of psychedelic biomechanicals to stimulate visionary experience. These essays make a strong case for the use of these substances in future religious practice."

FRANK BARRON, PH.D., SC.D., AUTHOR OF
NO ROOTLESS FLOWER: AN ECOLOGY OF CREATIVITY

"If you want more than emotional and subjective outpourings about entheogens, and if you think like I do that unless we expand our awareness we will not have a happy future, then this is a book to read."

RABBI ZALMAN M. SCHACHTER-SHALOMI,
AUTHOR OF *FROM AGE-ING TO SAGE-ING*

"Offers a thoughtful, sane examination of a topic of great social, psychological, and religious significance."

ROGER WALSH, M.D., PH.D., PROFESSOR OF
PSYCHIATRY AT THE UNIVERSITY OF CALIFORNIA

"Essential reading for everyone concerned with spiritual, psychological, and social well-being. A fascinating and significant collection."

FRANCES VAUGHAN, PH.D., AUTHOR OF
SHADOWS OF THE SACRED AND *THE INWARD ARC*

ENTHEOGENS
and FUTURE
the
of RELIGION

EDITED BY ROBERT FORTE

Park Street Press
Rochester, Vermont • Toronto, Canada

Park Street Press
One Park Street
Rochester, Vermont 05767
www.ParkStPress.com

Park Street Press is a division of Inner Traditions International

Note to the Reader: The information provided in this book is for educational, historical, and cultural interest only and should not be construed as advocacy for the use or ingestion of entheogens. Neither the author nor the publisher assumes any responsibility for physical, psychological, or social consequences resulting from the ingestion of these substances or their derivatives.

Library of Congress Cataloging-in-Publication Data
Entheogens and the future of religion / edited by Robert Forte.
    p. cm.
  Summary: "A study of the importance of psychedelic plants and drugs in religion and society"—Provided by publisher.
  Includes bibliographical references and index.
  ISBN 978-1-59477-438-6 (pbk.) ISBN 978-1-59477-797-4 (e-book)
  1. Hallucinogenic drugs and religious experience. 2. Psychology and religion. 3. Psychotropic drugs. 4. Spiritual life. I. Forte, Robert, 1956–
  BL65.D7E58 2012
                                                                2011039799
Printed and bound in the United States by Lake Book Manufacturing, Inc.
The text stock is SFI certified. The Sustainable Forestry Initiative® program promotes sustainable forest management.

10 9 8 7 6 5 4 3 2 1

Text design and layout by Virginia Scott Bowman
This book was typeset in Garamond Premier Pro with Perpetua as the display typeface

To all our relations

Let it be known
there is a fountain
that was not made
by the hands of man.

HUNTER/GARCIA

CONTENTS

For this is the very problem that is obsessing me: although I see man crushed, asphyxiated, diminished by industrial civilization, I can't believe that he will degenerate, decline morally, and finally perish, completely sterile. I have a limitless confidence in the creative power of the human mind. It seems to me that man will succeed—if he wishes—in remaining free and creative, in any circumstance, cosmic or historical.

But how can the miracle be brought about? How can the sacramental dimension of existence be rediscovered? At this point, so much can be said: all the things that have existed we have not definitively lost; we find them again in our dreams and our longings. And the poets have kept them. This is to say nothing of the religious life, because the authenticity and depth of the religious life among my contemporaries seems to me a most mysterious problem. There must be a way out. Aldous Huxley proposes mescaline. . . . There would be a great deal to say on that score.

MIRCEA ELIADE, *NO SOUVENIRS*, 1977

I am not so foolish as to equate what happens under the influence of mescalin or of any other drug, prepared or in the future preparable, with the realization of the end and ultimate purpose of human life: Enlightenment, the Beatific Vision. All I am suggesting is that the mescalin experience is what Catholic Theologians call "a gratuitous grace," not necessary to salvation but potentially helpful and to be accepted thankfully, if made available. To be shaken out of the ruts of ordinary perception, to be shown for a few timeless hours the outer and inner world, not as they appear to an animal obsessed with survival or to a human being obsessed with words and notions, but as they are apprehended, directly and unconditionally, by Mind at Large—this is an experience of inestimable value to anyone. . . .

ALDOUS HUXLEY,
THE DOORS OF PERCEPTION, 1954

FOREWORD TO
THE NEW EDTION
Robert Jesse

THE WORD "RELIGION" invites us to consider phenomena that arise and unfold over generations and centuries. Against this enduring backdrop, only a short space of time has elapsed since *Entheogens and the Future of Religion* first appeared in 1997. Subsequent to its initial publication, travelers along entheogenic paths have passed several milestones. I will summarize some of them here, focusing on the classical hallucinogens, such as psilocybin mushrooms or the peyote cactus, used to facilitate experiences of non-dual or unity consciousness.

SCIENCE

At the Johns Hopkins University, a team of investigators (of whom I am one) have conducted controlled experiments with psilocybin and healthy volunteers (instead of patients seeking medical or psychiatric treatment). The findings, published in 2006, 2008, and 2011,[1] confirm what the literature has long suggested: psilocybin, used under suitable conditions, frequently brings about experiences similar to mystical breakthroughs that occur spontaneously or through prolonged spiritual practice.[2] People who had such experiences in the research setting more often than not attributed great significance to them, ranking them among the top experiences of their lives. Additionally, most of these individuals reported positive changes in mood, outlook, and behavior, which friends and family members tended to corroborate.

Concurrently, research in positive psychology and behavioral economics has enhanced our understanding of traits and behavior patterns such as happiness and cooperation. These threads of inquiry are intertwining in another psilocybin study now underway at Johns Hopkins, which is looking at the outcomes of psilocybin sessions in combination with other spiritual practices.

Several institutions are following yet another line of research: examining the potential value of entheogen-induced transformative experiences in helping to relieve psychological distress in patients with life-threatening illnesses. The investigators are reporting that some of these patients have found the experiences to be enormously helpful.

LAW

Over the course of a century, U.S. law has come to accommodate one racial group practicing one religion using one forbidden substance, namely, the Native American use of peyote. Until recently no such accommodation has been made for other religious groups using any other entheogen on the federal list of controlled substances. That changed with a civil suit brought in federal court by the U.S. branch of a Brazilian religion, the União do Vegetal (UdV), under the Religious Freedom Restoration Act (RFRA) of 1993. The church's case—involving the use of ayahuasca, a plant mixture originating in Amazonia and containing DMT and other active chemicals—rose to the U.S. Supreme Court, which in 2006 issued an 8–0 ruling mostly favorable to the church.[3] Further laborious negotiations with the government have settled the conditions under which the UdV is now allowed to import and use its sacrament.

In 2008, a branch of the Santo Daime church in Ashland, Oregon, petitioned to stop the federal government from interfering in its practice of ayahuasca use. The district court, following the precedent in the UdV case, granted the request. The government has appealed—not to challenge again the church's right to use the substance, but to argue that officials should have the power to regulate that use.

The Religious Freedom Restoration Act requires the courts to determine on a case-by-case basis whether there is a "compelling government interest" in enforcing a federal law that burdens religion and to determine the "least restrictive means" of satisfying government interests. We can expect more cases involving religious liberty and entheogens to move through the courts successfully. It is possible that at some point administrative agencies will tire of losing in court and will create a streamlined process to accommodate religious use of these substances.

CULTURE

The prevalence of the Internet in today's society offers the appearance—which may reflect an actual trend—of an increasing interest in hallucinogens for therapeutic, creative, and spiritual purposes. Numerous online communities and websites, such as erowid.org, have emerged, which are allowing an unprecedented flow of entheogen-related information and advice.

Among the psychoactives used with explicit entheogenic intention, ayahuasca is becoming increasingly prominent. More scientific and anthropological publications about the sacramental brew are appearing, more South American ayahuasca practitioners are visiting North America and Europe, and more ayahuasca retreats are being offered around the world.

National Surveys on Drug Use and Health have indicated that more than 650,000 people a year in the United States used a hallucinogen (not including MDMA) for the first time.[4] How much of that use stems from a well-formed intention to receive insights or a well-formed commitment to spiritual growth? How often are the amounts ingested large enough to be likely to occasion mystical-type experiences? How often is that use adequately safeguarded and supported? How often do initiates have an opportunity to practice within the context of a healthy, stable community of seekers? Sometimes, surely, but probably not often.

Perhaps that explains why a net increase in saintly qualities is not immediately apparent, as one might hope, if great numbers of initiates each year are having unitive visions in social contexts that are nurturing ones. Perhaps this is yet to come, for the trend lines of science, law, and culture point toward more open and more fruitful use of these remarkable substances. In part because the entheogens make it practical to conduct experimental studies of non-dual consciousness and its consequences, we may see increased interest in other avenues of exploration, such as meditation, toward the same ends. It also remains to be seen whether and how the established non-entheogenic religions will respond to these developments. Will they come to devote more attention to the primary religious experience?

Meanwhile, for those who wish to explore the entheogenic waters, wisdom is freshly available. Gems among many include the books *Cleansing the Doors of Perception* by Huston Smith (Tarcher/Putnam 2000), *The Psychedelic Explorer's Guide* by James Fadiman (Park Street Press 2011), and the volume you are now holding.

For this compendium, my deep appreciation goes out to its contributors; to the staff at Inner Traditions, including Anne Dillon, Jon Graham, and Jeanie Levitan, for producing this edition; and to Robert Forte for his recognition of the importance of the subject and for gathering and shaping the book's material.

ROBERT JESSE
OCCIDENTAL, CALIFORNIA
SEPTEMBER 2011

Robert Jesse, convenor of the Council on Spiritual Practices, was trained in engineering at the Johns Hopkins University. He has worked in software development as an independent consultant and in several capacities for Oracle Corporation, most recently as a vice president for business development. In 1994 Bob began a leave of absence from Oracle to devote himself to the council's work. Since 1997 he has advanced scientific studies and coauthored papers on the psychospiritual effects of psilocybin.

NOTES

1. www.csp.org/psilocybin.
2. www.csp.org/PRE.
3. www.udvusa.com.
4. National Survey on Drug Use and Health. *Patterns of Hallucinogen Use and Initiation: 2004 and 2005.* Rockville, Md.: Substance Abuse and Mental Health Services Administration, 2007.

ACKNOWLEDGMENTS

THIS COLLECTION GREW out of a symposium in Big Sur, California, that was inspired and supported by many folks, especially Stuart Abelson, Mircea Eliade, Stan and Christina Grof, and Dick Price. Many dear friends, guides, and inspiring (and patient) teachers appeared along the way to the book's final form. Frank Barron and Claudio Naranjo watched the entire process unfold and I hope are pleased with the result. Jan Krinsley, Kelly Simmons, and Peter Stafford helped in the early preparation of the manuscript. Bob Wallace and Bob Jesse played key roles in bringing it all together and to you. Thanks for loving and critical support to Michael Abbott, Greg Bogart, Brooks Cole, Clark Heinrich, Minh-Hang Nguyen, and Dale Pendell. Thank you Nina Graboi, beloved psychedelic godmother. Thank you Jaime. And thank you Timothy, wherever you are. A by-no-means-final debt of gratitude is owed to the worldwide entheogen community—those who keep the flame burning, sometimes at great peril and personal sacrifice.

FIAT LUX

—ROBERT FORTE,
EDITOR

The Worm's Waking

This is how a human being can change:
there's a worm addicted to eating
grape leaves.

Suddenly, he wakes up,
call it grace, whatever, something
wakes him, and he's no longer
a worm.

He's the entire vineyard,
and the orchard too, the fruit, the trunks,
a growing wisdom and joy
that doesn't need
to devour.

JALALUDDIN RUMI, THIRTEENTH CENTURY,
FROM *THE ESSENTIAL RUMI*,
TRANSLATED BY COLEMAN BARKS

INTRODUCTION
Robert Forte

Robert Forte, an independent scholar of entheogens, psychology, and religion, also edited *Timothy Leary: Outside Looking In* (Park Street Press 1999) and the thirtieth anniversary edition of *The Road to Eleusis: Unveiling the Secret of the Mysteries* (North Atlantic Books 2008). A former director of the Albert Hofmann Foundation, he teaches at the California Institute of Integral Studies and is studying the effects of cannabis, ayahuasca, and other natural medicines on cancer. http://ciis.academia.edu/RobertForte.

THE TERM *ENTHEOGEN* was introduced into the English language in 1979 to refer to plants or chemical substances that awaken or generate mystical experiences (Ruck et al. 1979). It is used here in the spirit of its conception to distinguish the religious nature of these substances and the experiences they evoke from their effects in other contexts, for which there are other terms, psychedelic or hallucinogen. Once, when a journalist casually referred to peyote (a classic entheogen) as a drug, a Huichol Indian shaman replied, "Aspirin is a drug, peyote is sacred."

We live in a time when a great many voices are calling for a spiritual renewal to help us address some of the problems that face humanity. The great spiritual theologian Matthew Fox is one such voice. He

1

wrote, "At a National Academy of Sciences conference in 1986 exploring the mass extinction of plants and animals on our planet, Paul R. Ehrlich of Stanford University declared, 'Scientific analysis points, curiously, toward the need for a quasi-religious transformation of contemporary cultures'" (Fox 1988, 2).

Yet the way of the entheogens—one of the oldest and most widespread means of attaining a religious experience—is forbidden, surrounded by a miasma of controversy and misunderstanding. This problem was further complicated during the 1970s, '80s, and '90s by a "war on drugs" waged to eradicate the illicit, recreational, non-medical "abuse" of drugs. Entheogens have been swept up in this official anti-drug crusade even though they differ considerably from, and do not rank highly among, drugs of abuse. In fact, these substances, when used in a context to educe spiritual awareness, have been used with some success to alleviate addictions to narcotic drugs and alcohol. No less an authority than William G. Wilson, founder of Alcoholics Anonymous, observed, "Though LSD and some kindred alkaloids have had an amazingly bad press, there seems to be no doubt of their immense and growing value" (Forte 1999, 244).

This is one of the most mysterious and important subjects in all religious history. Entheogens have figured prominently in the mystical practices of some of the world's greatest civilizations. They have been widely employed in shamanic societies, and their use continues today throughout the world. They alter consciousness in such a profound way that, depending on the set and setting, their effects can range from states resembling psychosis to what are perhaps the ultimate human experiences: union with God or revelation of other mystical realities. Though they affect the psyche so powerfully, entheogens are among the biologically safest drugs known.

At the present time, nearly all the entheogens are listed in the Controlled Substance Act of the United States as having "no medical use and a high potential for abuse" and are thereby subject to the most stringent controls. Criminal penalties punish unsanctioned use—and virtually no use is sanctioned. Though it is technically possible for medical research proposals to be approved by the government, the process of applying for permission is long, expensive, and for researchers with temporal and fiscal constraints, prohibitive. In a survey of former psychedelic researchers, the late Walter Houston Clark, professor emeritus of the psychology of religion at Andover Newton Theological Seminary, found that governmental red tape was the primary reason why they had ceased working in this field. "It would seem that something is wrong if qualified investigators find it so difficult to obtain funds and permission to work in an area that most feel will open important doors to the future of humanity" (Clark 1975, 15).

To some extent this problem can be attributed to the behavior of Timothy Leary (1920–1996), who took it upon himself to be a cheerleader for the cause of psychedelics—against the wishes of some of his colleagues at the time. Among them, Frank Barron, Aldous Huxley, Huston Smith, and others felt that these materials were sacred and urged that they be treated with discretion and respect as was accorded the sacrament at Eleusis, alchemical elixirs, and the like. Unwilling or unable to contain his enthusiasm, Leary popularized psychedelic drugs in the 1960s and identified them as catalysts of a revolutionary social movement. He encouraged their use in ways that were seen as (and often were) hedonistic, irresponsible, or radically threatening to the status quo, thereby provoking the restrictive legislation we see today.

But psychedelic drug prohibition existed long before Leary. A persistent and often violent repression of entheogens commonly occurred when they were encountered by European colonialists in their conquest of the New World, to such an extent that they might have been lost for all time. Were it not for the painstaking research of Valentina and Gordon Wasson, the serendipitous discovery of LSD by Albert Hofmann in 1938, and Aldous Huxley's description of his mescaline experience in *The Doors of Perception* in 1954, this repression may have succeeded entirely. Leary's efforts assured that entheogens would not be forgotten again anytime soon. Millions were inspired by his zeal to explore these remarkable materials, and as a result, some of the leading minds of the '60s generation were enriched by them. The 1993 Nobel

Laureate Kary Mullis has gone so far as to say, "I think I might have been stupid in some respects, if it weren't for my psychedelic experiences" (Mullis 1995).

However, the sudden impact of entheogens upon a predominantly secular and materialistic society left no time for the appropriate educational, religious, or medical agencies to understand or accommodate their effects. Laws designed to protect citizens were counterproductive. They effectively curtailed professional research while having the opposite effect on an underground society. The result is that many otherwise law-abiding citizens continue to use these substances in secret for fear of prosecution. The dangers of the entheogens are exaggerated by ignorance, and their potential virtues remain hidden.

Direct experience of the divine is a goal of spiritual seekers everywhere. But without the proper framework to understand mystical experience, even glorious encounters with the divine can be problematic or confusing. By contrast, difficult experiences that occur within the context of a religious model can be valuable and transformative. In societies where ecstatic experiences are successfully integrated, it is because a suitable framework exists to define or structure them. Mircea Eliade considers this an "essential element" in understanding ecstasy.

> . . . we must keep in mind the two essential elements of the problem: on the one hand, the ecstatic experience as a primary phenomenon; on the other, the historico-religious milieu into which this ecstatic experience was destined to be incorporated and the ideology that, in the last analysis, was to validate it. We have termed the ecstatic experience a "primary phenomenon" because we see no reason whatever for regarding it as the result of a particular historical moment. Rather we would consider it as fundamental in the human condition, and hence known to the whole of archaic humanity; what changed and was modified with the different forms of culture and religion was the interpretation and evaluation of the ecstatic experience. (Eliade 1964, 504)

Unfortunately today the "interpretation and evaluation" of the entheogenic ecstatic experience have been determined exclusively by a medical-psychiatric paradigm that generally is not oriented toward appreciating mystical states of consciousness. This "paradigm problem" has been vigorously enunciated by Stanislav Grof, M.D., who, after twenty-five years of research, concluded that "neither the nature of the LSD experience nor the numerous observations made in the course of psychedelic therapy can be adequately explained in terms of the Newtonian-Cartesian, mechanistic approach to the universe" (Grof 1985, 31). And, as Daniel X. Freedman, M.D., president of the American Psychiatric Association, said in 1983 when asked about the possibility of resuming research into the therapeutic effectiveness of psychedelics, "Psychedelic drugs have not demonstrated sufficient relevance to the health service concerns of the psychiatric profession; but this is the most interesting subject I have encountered in all my years of science. Religion, that's the field for them" (Freedman 1983). It seems right then to turn to other disciplines, mainly religion—but also to psychology, philosophy, phenomenology, and art—to explore their value.

These writings aim to direct attention to the distinctly sacred nature of these substances with the hope that religious-minded investigators, policy architects, and the concerned public will take note. It is our hope that this book will contribute to an honest reappraisal of the historic and modern significance of entheogens so that they may be used accordingly in today's world by those seeking to cultivate their spiritual awareness.

Since this book was first published by the Council on Spiritual Practices in 1997, we've seen many positive changes in the world of entheogens, as Robert Jesse describes in his foreword to this new edition. At the same time it must be said that monumental changes, not for the better, have occurred in contemporary American society and throughout the world.

The environmental crisis, urgent at the time of our first publication, has worsened. Politically, there have been sweeping changes that have undermined the democracy of the United States, following the terrorist attacks of 9/11 (Wolf 2007; www.globalresearch.ca). Although a great many of the world's most prominent government officials, military officers, scientists, and philosophers present strong evidence that 9/11 has not been legally adjudicated and that the official story is preposterously false, nonetheless the attacks are used to justify the longest, most destructive, and most expensive wars in U.S. history, which at present show no sign of abating (Griffin 2011). Indeed it seems, as former Secretary of Defense Donald Rumsfeld says, we have entered a period of endless war. Largely as a result of these wars, at the time of this writing, the world stands on the precipice of a global economic collapse, worse than the Great Depression (www.rawstory.com/rs/2011).

Yet, crisis may equal opportunity. Many contributors to this volume describe how the intelligent use of entheogens could inspire peaceful, sustainable responses to the catastrophic state of modern society. The plot is thickening. Can the human species reverse these unfortunate developments of modernity?

Don't speak too soon, for the wheels are still spinning.

When the Waters Were Changed

Once upon a time Khidr, the teacher of Moses, called upon mankind with a warning. At a certain date, he said, all the water in the world which had not been specially hoarded, would disappear. It would then be renewed, with different water, which would drive men mad.

Only one man listened to the meaning of this advice. He collected water and went to a secure place where he stored it, and waited for the water to change its character. On the appointed date the streams stopped running, the wells went dry, and the man who had listened, seeing this happening, went to his retreat and drank his preserved water. When he saw, from his security, the waterfalls again beginning to flow, this man descended among the other sons of men. He found that they were thinking and talking in an entirely different way from before; yet they had no memory of what had happened, nor of having been warned. When he tried to talk to them, he realized that they thought that he was mad, and they showed hostility or compassion, not understanding.

At first, he drank none of the new water, but went back to his concealment, to draw on his supplies, every day. Finally, however, he took the decision to drink the new water because he could not bear the loneliness of living, behaving and thinking in a different way from everyone else. He drank the new water, and became like the rest. Then he forgot all about his own store of special water, and his fellows began to look upon him as a madman who had miraculously been restored to sanity.

A NINTH-CENTURY SUFI TALE

REFERENCES

"Can Religion Save Us?" www.enlightennext.org/magazine/j23/smith.asp?page=2.

Clark, W. H. "Psychedelic Research: Obstacles and Values." *Journal of Humanistic Psychology* 15 (3) (1975).

Eliade, M. *Shamanism: Archaic Techniques of Ecstasy.* Princeton, N.J.: Bollingen Series, 1964.

Forte, R. *Timothy Leary, Outside Looking In: Appreciations, Castigations, Reminiscences.* Rochester, Vt.: Park Street Press, 1999.

Fox, M. *The Coming of the Cosmic Christ.* San Francisco: HarperSanFrancisco, 1988.

Freedman, D. X. Personal communication. 1983.

Griffin, David Ray. *9/11 Ten Years Later: When State Crimes against Democracy Succeed.* New York: Olive Branch Press, 2011.

Grof, S. *Beyond the Brain.* Albany, N.Y.: State University of New York Press, 1985.

Mullis, K. Quotation in *MAPS Bulletin* 5 (3) (1995): 53.

Ruck, C. A. P., et al. "Entheogens." *Journal of Psychedelic Drugs* 11 (1–2) (1979): 145–46.

Scott, Peter Dale. "Supplanting the United States Constitution: War, National Emergency, and Continuity of Government," www.globalresearch.ca/PrintArticle.php?article/d=19238.

Webster, Stephen C., "IMF Adviser: The Global Ecomony Could Collapse in Two Weeks to Three Weeks." www.rawstory.com.

Wolf, Naomi. *The End of America: Letter of Warning to a Young Patriot.* White River Junction, Vt.: Chelsea Green Publishing, 2007.

1 TESTIMONY OF THE COUNCIL ON SPIRITUAL PRACTICES

Robert Jesse

Robert Jesse, convenor of the Council on Spiritual Practices, was trained in engineering at the Johns Hopkins University. He has worked in software development as an independent consultant and in several capacities for Oracle Corporation, most recently as a vice president for business development. In 1994 Bob began a leave of absence from Oracle to devote himself to the council's work. Since 1997 he has advanced scientific studies and coauthored papers on the psychospiritual effects of psilocybin.

To us in the Southwest, this freedom of religion has singular significance because it affects diverse cultures. It is as much of us as the rain on our hair, the wind on the grass, and the sun on our faces. It is so naturally a part of us that when the joy of this beautiful freedom sings in our souls, we find it hard to conceive that it could ever be imperiled. Yet, today, in this land of bright blue skies and yellow grass, of

9

dusty prairies and beautiful mesas, and vistas of red earth
with walls of weathered rock, eroded by oceans of time, the
free spirit of the individual once again is threatened. . . .
CHIEF JUDGE BURCIAGA, *UNITED STATES V. BOYLL,*
U.S. DISTRICT COURT, D.N.M., SEPTEMBER 3, 1991

An earlier version of this essay was presented to the Committee on Drugs
and the Law of the Association of the Bar of the City of New York on
October 10, 1995.

THE COUNCIL ON SPIRITUAL PRACTICES is concerned primarily with
religious experience and only secondarily with plants and chemicals or
policies toward them. The drug laws, by contrast, and the agencies that
enforce them, are concerned mostly with the substances and little with
the religious uses to which some are put. I invite you to consider the
impact that the drug laws inadvertently have on the free exercise of
religion, affecting people for whom certain prohibited substances are
an essential feature of their spiritual practices. That impact effectively
constitutes religious persecution, even though most of the people con-
ducting it have no desire to persecute and no idea that they are doing so.

THE ENTHEOGENS

The substances of interest here are those known in the medical community as hallucinogens and elsewhere as the psychedelics. These drugs
are sharply dissimilar from drugs such as cocaine and heroin; several
of them have been shown to be very low in addiction potential and
overdose risk (Gable 1993) and to be of very low organic toxicity. The
risks of injurious behavior and of psychological harm from the altered-
consciousness experience, which are not negligible in unsupervised
casual use, appear to be minimized when they are used in ritual settings
(Cohen 1960; Bergman 1971; Strassman 1984). It is the ability of these

substances to catalyze religious experience that is of interest to CSP; to emphasize this, we use the word *entheogen,* coined from Greek roots signifying "to realize the divine within" (Ott 1993, 103–5), to describe them when used for spiritual purposes.

For as long as we know of, there have been at least a few people in every culture, the mystics and the saints, who were able through prayer, meditation, or other techniques to bring upon themselves mystical states of consciousness (James 1958), also called *primary religious experience.* In some cultures, this direct experience of the sacred was available to everyone, or to members of special bodies of initiates, through the sacramental use of psychoactive plants and preparations. There is now substantial evidence that the Eleusinian Mystery rites, performed annually near Athens for almost two thousand years, featured a mystical revelation brought on by the drinking of an entheogenic brew (Wasson, Ruck, and Hofmann 1978). The Sanskrit *Rig Veda,* one of the oldest religious texts known, praises a mind-altering substance called *soma,* which Wasson (1968) identified as the psychoactive mushroom *Amanita muscaria.* Both in the New World and in the Old, ritual use has long been made of another class of entheogenic mushrooms: those containing psilocybin. In Mesoamerica, the entheogenic cactus peyote was used in spiritual practices as early as 300 B.C.E. To this day, indigenous peoples in Russia, Africa, Mexico, South America, and North America, including an estimated 250,000 to 400,000 American Indians in the United States (Franklin and Patchen 1994), use a variety of psychoactive sacraments classified as Schedule I controlled substances in the United States. I will return to the Native Americans presently.

Over the last century, as Western ethnobotanists rediscovered some of the traditional sacramental substances and as chemists isolated their active principles, this knowledge slowly circulated among the intelligentsia. Aldous Huxley took mescaline, the principal psychoactive component of peyote, in 1953 and described his awakening experience in *The Doors of Perception.* By that time, another wave had been set in motion. In 1943, Albert Hofmann (1983) discovered the psychoactivity of LSD.

Within a few decades, potent chemical means for facilitating primary religious experience were within easy reach of many people. It must be acknowledged that probably most contemporary users of hallucinogens take them with no explicit ritual surround or spiritual intention, though even then, the fire from heaven has been known to descend unbidden.

The religious import of the entheogens is confirmed in accounts by and of religious leaders and members of traditional entheogen-using cultures (Furst 1972, 1976; Schultes and Hofmann 1979; Dobkin de Rios 1984). This spiritual significance is corroborated by the accounts of scores of Western authorities (Metzner 1968; Roberts and Hruby 1995), including physician and church founder John Aiken (1970); Walter Houston Clark (1969), professor of psychology of religion at Andover Newton Theological Seminary; Harvard theologian Harvey Cox (1977); retired MIT philosopher and scholar of comparative religion Huston Smith (1964, 1992); Jesuit scholar David Toolan (1987); and David M. Wulff, professor of psychology of religion at Wheaton College (1991). A landmark scientific study, the "Good Friday Experiment" conducted under the sponsorship of Harvard University by physician and minister Walter Pahnke in 1962, also strongly supports the thesis that the entheogens facilitate mystical consciousness and are compatible with Christian worship (Pahnke 1963; Pahnke and Richards 1969; Doblin 1991).

RELIGIOUS LIBERTY

In the religious persecutions of the European early modern age, whether the struggle was Catholic against Lutheran, Calvinist against Anabaptist, or Anglican against Unitarian, the central issues tended to concern the efficacy of various sacraments. The same issue has resurfaced in the suppression of entheogenic practices. It is not surprising that people take very seriously disagreements about what can actually bring them closer to the divine. But Americans decided two centuries ago that such arguments are too important to be settled by force or by majority vote (Madison 1787). They are best left to the decisions of spiritual communities or to the individual conscience.

The First Amendment to the Constitution and a variety of statutes, administrative practices, and judicial decisions all protect religious freedom in this country. The fundamental principles of that corpus of law are that 1) the state may not treat any particular religion preferentially and that 2) you can live your religious life pretty much as you choose so long as you don't infringe the rights of others or interfere too much with essential public interests.

The entheogens present a complex problem for those who want to make good on our nation's promise of religious liberty. The classical form of religious persecution involves banning certain activities expressly because of their religious intent or content. That kind of persecution is relatively easy to identify and remedy. With entheogens, the present burden on religion comes in the form of a general ban on substances that are sometimes used spiritually and sometimes not. To relieve the burden, an exemption must be granted from the laws of general applicability that impose the burden.

NATIVE AMERICAN USE OF PEYOTE

This complex problem has been thoroughly explored in the instance of the Native American sacramental use of peyote. As the peyote religion spread among tribes in the United States in the late 1800s, it was met with explicit government persecution in the form of rules forbidding Indian use of peyote and, for example, "old heathenish dances." Since then, numerous contradictory federal and state legislative, regulatory, enforcement, and court actions have variously supported and denied Indian use of peyote (Peregoy, Echo-Hawk, and Botsford 1995).

The most prominent failure to accommodate this religious practice was the 1990 Supreme Court decision in *Employment Division v. Smith,* which ruled that the First Amendment does not protect the use of peyote by Native Americans. The court reached its decision by changing prior standards to make it much harder to get relief from laws of general applicability that burden religious activity. A broad coalition of religious bodies responded swiftly by advocating new federal legislation, leading to the enactment of the Religious Freedom Restoration Act of 1993 (PL 103–141; Carmella 1995). Finally, in 1994, the federal government enacted the American Indian Religious Freedom Act Amendments (PL 103–344), providing consistent protection across all fifty states for the traditional, ceremonial use of peyote by American Indians.

What price, if any, does society pay for the granting of this religious liberty? The House of Representatives Committee on Natural Resources reported, "Medical evidence, based on the opinion of scientists and other experts, including medical doctors and anthropologists, is that peyote is not injurious" (HR 103–675 1994, 7). Indeed, with a long history of use and several hundred thousand people currently active in the Native American Church, the incidence of peyote-related harm appears to be vanishingly small (Bergman 1971). What is more, the committee also reported, "Spiritual and social support provided by the Native American Church has been effective in combating the tragic effects of alcoholism among the Native American population."

ACCOMMODATING
OTHER ENTHEOGEN PRACTICES

So United States law now accommodates one racial group practicing one religion using one controlled substance. Yet there are also non-Indian religious groups and individuals in this country for whom entheogens play a central sacramental role. They are less well known at least in part because, in the absence of protections, their worship potentially subjects them to fines, forfeitures, and imprisonment. How could we respond to a non-Indian group that wishes to use peyote in its religious practices? Or to a group that wants to use some other plant or chemical for similar purposes?

It is possible to hold the view that people ought to be permitted to use some controlled substances for religious purposes without holding the libertarian view that everyone ought to be able to use any drug for any purpose. On a more practical level, one can believe that it is safe for people to take peyote and therefore to permit peyote taking, without also believing that another drug is safe and should be available.

Thus, the right to free exercise of religion could be honored by granting narrow exemptions for the use of only some substances in carefully circumscribed religious contexts. Such exemptions would support the anti-drug-abuse objectives of the current drug laws. If a religious group without a demonstrated safety record were to seek an exemption, government might reasonably ask a number of questions, for example:

- Is the group working with a substance of reasonable safety?
- Does it draw a reasonably sharp line between ritual and recreational use?
- How is informed consent obtained?
- What safeguards does it incorporate in its practices to protect participants?
- What is its policy regarding minors?

One accommodation mechanism would be to allow applicants to document their proposed entheogen use and, if they satisfy reasonable safety requirements, receive an exemption. This could be done at the denominational level or by licensing qualified "entheogen practitioners," who would then serve spiritual communities or individuals. Licensees would grow or obtain, store, and be accountable for the supervised use of the authorized substances. Simple record-keeping practices would enable monitoring of the prevalence and safety of entheogen use and the need for any policy adjustments as necessary.

These are very important details, ones that CSP is addressing—but they are details. The main question we ask you to consider is whether the current laws, which forbid all Americans except Indians to use scheduled psychoactive sacraments, are justifiable in light of constitutional traditions and a realistic assessment of the risks associated with the entheogens.*

QUOTES WITHOUT COMMENT

I have argued that every human being is born with an innate drive to experience altered states of consciousness periodically—in particular to learn how to get away from ordinary ego-centered consciousness. I have also explained my intuition that this drive is a most important factor in our evolution, both as individuals and as a species. Nonordinary experiences are vital to us because they are expressions of our unconscious minds, and the integration of conscious and unconscious experience is the key to life, health, and spiritual development, and fullest use of our nervous systems.

ANDREW WEIL, M.D.,
THE NATURAL MIND, 1972

"There is evidence that spirituality is an element in recovery from addiction," said Dr. William Miller, research director for the Center on Alcoholism, Substance Abuse and Addiction at the University of New Mexico.

Dr. Miller cited data on how AA members who make strong commitments to the spiritual basis of the program gain sufficient "meaning in life" to displace the need for alcohol.

---

*This is beginning to change. See the section titled "Law" on page xii of this book; www
.udvusa.com; www. ayahuasca.com; and www.bialabate.net.

AA founder Bill Wilson, an alcoholic himself, started the movement after being freed from alcohol craving by a sudden religious experience one day in the 1930s in New York.

LARRY WITHAM, "PHYSICIANS RESEARCH
RELIGIOUS ECSTASY AS CURE FOR ADDICTS,"
THE WASHINGTON TIMES, SUNDAY, APRIL 23, 1995

Bill [Wilson, founder of AA] first took LSD . . . August 29, 1956. . . . Bill was enthusiastic about his experience; he felt it helped him eliminate many barriers erected by the self, or ego, that stand in the way of one's direct experience of the cosmos and of God. He thought he might have found something that could make a big difference to the lives of many who still suffered.

ALCOHOLICS ANONYMOUS, *PASS IT ON:*
THE STORY OF BILL WILSON AND HOW THE
A.A. MESSAGE REACHED THE WORLD, 1984

We are aware of man's fallibility and will be protected in our studies by that understanding and recognition of the First Cause of all created things and the laws that govern them.

We therefore approach the study of these psychodelics [sic] and their influence in the mind of man anxious to discover whatever attributes they possess, respectfully evaluating their proper place in the Divine Economy.

We humbly ask Our Heavenly Mother the Virgin Mary, help of all who call upon Her to aid us to know and understand the true qualities of these psychodelics [sic], the full capacities of man's noblest faculties and according to God's laws to use them for the benefit of mankind here and in eternity.

MONSIGNOR J. E. BROWN, "INTRODUCTION TO
LSD EXPERIENCE," CATHEDRAL OF THE HOLY ROSARY,
ARCHDIOCESE OF BRITISH COLUMBIA,
DECEMBER 8, 1957

REFERENCES

Aiken, J. W. "The Church of the Awakening." In *Psychedelics: The Uses and Implications of Hallucinogenic Drugs.* Edited by B. Aaronson and H. Osmond. New York: Anchor Books, 1970.

Bergman, R. L. "Navajo Peyote Use: Its Apparent Safety." *American Journal of Psychiatry* 128 (6) (1971): 695–99.

Carmella, A. C. "The Religious Freedom Restoration Act." *Religion & Values in Public Life* 3 (2) (1995).

Clark, W. H. *Chemical Ecstasy.* New York: Sheed & Ward, 1969.

Cohen, S. "Lysergic Acid Diethylamide: Side Effects and Complications." *Journal of Nervous and Mental Disease* 130 (1) (1960).

Cox, H. *Turning East: The Promise and Peril of the New Orientalism.* New York: Simon and Schuster, 1977.

Dobkin de Rios, M. *Hallucinogens: Cross-cultural Perspectives.* Albuquerque: University of New Mexico Press, 1984.

Doblin, R. Pahnke. "'Good Friday Experiment': A Long-term Follow-up and Methodological Critique." *Journal of Transpersonal Psychology* (23) (1991): 1.

Franklin, V., and J. D. Patchen. "The Jurisprudence of Peyote in the United States." *The Entheogen Law Reporter,* Winter 1994.

Furst, P. T. *Flesh of the Gods: The Ritual Use of Hallucinogens.* Prospect Heights, Ill.: Waveland Press, 1972.

———. *Hallucinogens and Culture.* Novato, Calif.: Chandler & Sharp, 1976.

Gable, R. S. "Toward a Comparative Overview of Dependence Potential and Acute Toxicity of Psychoactive Substances Used Nonmedically." *American Journal of Drug and Alcohol Abuse* 19 (3) (1993): 263–81.

Hofmann, A. *LSD: My Problem Child.* Los Angeles: J. P. Tarcher, 1983.

House of Representatives, Committee on Natural Resources. *American Indian Religious Freedom Act Amendments of 1994* (report). HR 103–675.

Huxley, A. *The Doors of Perception.* London: Chatto & Windus, 1954.

James, W. *The Varieties of Religious Experience.* New York: New American Library, 1958.

Madison, J. "Federalist No. 10." In *The Federalist Papers.* Edited by C. Rossiter. New York: Signet Classics, 1787.

Metzner, R., ed. *The Ecstatic Adventure.* New York: Macmillan, 1968.

Ott, J. *Pharmacotheon.* Occidental, Calif.: Natural Products Co., 1993.

Pahnke, W. N. "Drugs and Mysticism: An Analysis of the Relationship between Psychedelic Drugs and the Mystical Consciousness." Ph.D. diss., Harvard University, 1963.

Pahnke, W. N., and W. A. Richards. "Implications of LSD and Experimental Mysticism." *Journal of Transpersonal Psychology* 1 (2) (1969).

Peregoy, R. M., W. R. Echo-Hawk, and J. Botsford. "Congress Overturns Supreme Court's Peyote Ruling." *NARF Legal Review* 20 (1) (1995).

Roberts, T. B., and P. J. Hruby. *Religion and Psychoactive Sacraments: A Bibliographic Guide.* San Francisco: Council on Spiritual Practices, 1995.

Schultes, R. E., and A. Hofmann. *Plants of the Gods.* New York: McGraw-Hill, 1979.

Smith, H. "Do Drugs Have Religious Import?" *The Journal of Philosophy* 61 (18) (1964).

———. *Forgotten Truth: The Common Vision of the World's Religions.* San Francisco: HarperSanFrancisco, 1992.

Strassman, R. J. "Adverse Reactions to Psychedelic Drugs: A Review of the Literature." *Journal Nervous and Mental Disease* 172 (10) (1984): 577–95.

Toolan, D. *Facing West from California Shores: A Jesuit's Journey into New Age Consciousness.* New York: Crossroad, 1987.

Wasson, R. G. *Soma: Divine Mushroom of Immortality.* New York: Harcourt Brace Jovanovich, 1968.

Wasson, R. G., C. A. P. Ruck, and A. Hofmann. *The Road to Eleusis.* New York: Harcourt Brace Jovanovich, 1978.

Watts, A. *The Joyous Cosmology: Adventures in the Chemistry of Consciousness.* New York: Pantheon, 1962.

Wulff, D. M. *Psychology of Religion: Classic and Contemporary Views.* New York: John Wiley & Sons, 1991.

2 EXPLORATIONS INTO GOD

Brother David Steindl-Rast

Brother David Steindl-Rast, Ph.D., O.S.B., was born in Vienna where he studied art, anthropology, and psychology. After receiving a Ph.D. from the University of Vienna, he joined the Benedictine Monastery of Mount Saviour. After twelve years of monastic training and studies in philosophy and theology, Brother David received Vatican approval in 1967 to participate in a Christian-Buddhist dialogue with Zen teachers Hakuun Yasutani Roshi, Shunryu Suzuki Roshi, Soen Nakagawa Roshi, and Eido Shimano Roshi. Together with Thomas Merton, Brother David contributed to the renewal of religious life, especially through the House of Prayer Movement of the 1970s.

His books have been translated into many languages. *Gratefulness, the Heart of Prayer* and *A Listening Heart* have been reprinted and anthologized for well over a decade. Brother David has coauthored *Belonging to the Universe,* a dialogue on new paradigm thinking in science and theology, with physicist Fritjof Capra, and *The Ground We Share,* a book on Buddhist and Christian practice, with Robert Aitken Roshi. In 1996, after thirty years as a writer, retreat master, and lecturer, Brother David received permission to return to full-time monastic seclusion.

So many are grabbing for the money, so many
Want a free lunch, or are cynical and settle
For entertainment, that the world has adopted
Shallowness as its habit, and what was once

Our birthright is now considered deviation.
So squandered is our natural wisdom, that he
Who seeks the source of the flowing itself,
—the Muse's spring—is thought a fool:

Who really desires laurel, or myrtle either?
"Goddess-lover, go, in the rags you deserve!"
Is what they'll say, themselves pursuing

More material gains. You'll find few comrades
On your chosen path; but for that reason I pray
All the more that you will not falter.

PETRARCH, FOURTEENTH CENTURY,
THE RIME SPARSE, TRANSLATED BY DALE PENDELL

For two weeks in December 1984, forty-five scientists and religious thinkers gathered at Esalen Institute in Big Sur, California, to discuss ways to better understand the psychedelic experience. Brother David Steindl-Rast came down from his mountain hermitage and gave this extemporaneous talk.

A LOT WAS said this morning. Unfortunately, I only came last night. I was not here from the beginning of the conference. But what was said this morning really feels very comfortable. I think somehow I belong to this League for Spiritual Discovery.

The particular branch of the league that I belong to is fifteen hundred years old. That is how long we have been engaged on that *Voyage of Discovery* in Benedictine monasteries. From my own experience, for whatever that is worth, I give you my word: It works! The monastic experience in the form in which it is offered to us today (here in this country or in other parts of the world that I have seen) is one possibility for discovering the things that we are all about. That is a great thing to know.

Of course, institutions are institutions with all their drawbacks. The monastic institution has all the drawbacks of an institution that is in our case fifteen hundred years old. And so the institution can also get in the way of achieving the goal. But in the optimal case, it works and brings about what we are looking for. I have seen it happen. I have known monks who have gone through this process. In many other cases, it is no guarantee at all, and you can just waste your time in a monastery as you can waste your time anywhere else. You can hide behind the institution.

You can experience a kind of inoculation that Stan Grof spoke about. We have used that image ourselves. We have said that you can get little by little vaccinated against the Good News of Christ. So that the real thing does not hit you anymore. You have become immune to the great mind-blowing turnabout. That is a real danger. But if the monastic experience works, it can get you to our deepest sense of unity and to a life that flows out of it.

I thought I would briefly sketch how I see the relationship between *spirituality* and *religion* and *theology*—all terms that have been tossed around here. In my understanding of it, and from the particular perspective from which I come to it, it all starts with our mystical experience. This is one point where I would question how John Perry meant his statement. I wrote it down and tried to capture it verbatim: "It is impossible to convince the general public that there is such a reality as a mystical experience."

Now I question that. I have had the opportunity to address all kinds of "general public." Some of them were most unlikely to be convinced offhand that there is such a thing as a mystical experience, let alone that they themselves had one. But I have never come across a group in which the majority could not be led to realize that they had had a mystical experience. In fact, I am convinced that our typical awareness as humans, our human consciousness, is based on the mystical experience, i.e., *the experience that we unconditionally belong.* This is my way of expressing the essence of a mystical experience: *an overwhelming sense of unconditional belonging.* I would be very interested in hearing how some of you express the same thing from different perspectives.

I always try to speak about it in common human language, in terms that anybody can understand. First, I get people settled and willing to listen, willing to look at themselves. Then I ask them, "Does it make sense to you that before you are aware of anything else, you have a sense of belonging? Not necessarily before *in time,* but *ontologically.* Is that sense of belonging not the basis of your awareness *that you are* and *who you are*? Is not the rock bottom of your consciousness a sense of belonging?"

"Belonging." That is the term I use. And I would say that 99 percent of a typical audience agrees. The others are just a little uncertain if they have really understood. But there is no one who says, "No, this simply doesn't ring true." Almost everyone says "Yes." That is enough for me.

Mystical experience, mystical awareness, is practically universal when we focus on its essence, which is that sense of ultimate belonging. Of course, from here on there are many degrees of potential development. We can make progress in our sense of belonging. But it is healthy for us and helpful to remember that basically everybody shares that awareness. It is the one thing you can presuppose. There is nothing else you can presuppose with as much certainty among humans as mystical awareness.

It is not always crystallized in specific experiences, although surprisingly often even this is the case, and among unlikely candidates for a mystical experience. But at least the awareness is there. And from that awareness we come now to spirituality. By "spirituality" I mean that which makes a religion tick. I call it "spirituality" rather than "religion" to avoid confusion with "the religions." Think rather of that *religiousness* which makes a religion religious. Remember, a religion is not automatically religious. In fact, my contention is that *religions,* left to themselves, turn *irreligious.* They have a tendency to become irreligious. If you are a member of a religious community, you have the responsibility to make your religion religious. This will not happen without your special effort.

Once we come to distinguish religion (in the sense of religiousness) from the various religions in which religion expresses itself, then we have the context in which to introduce "God." For most of us this is not absolutely necessary. There are many deeply religious people who would not use the term "God." But if we want to use it, this is where the term "God" comes in.

In some respects it is easier to speak about these things without using the term "God." It lends itself to too many misunderstandings. But if we want to use it as a kind of shortcut, it is in the context of our mystical awareness that "God" comes in. For anybody who uses that term "God" will agree: *God is the one to whom we absolutely belong.* We are back at that sense of belonging.

Before you fill this notion of God with anything else, you can say, those who use the term "God" correctly mean by it the reference point of our sense of belonging. But with this sense of belonging goes a sense of longing. Check that out against your own experience.

Here this whole thing comes in motion. This is something I cannot explain further. It is an experiential fact. We long for that to which we most deeply belong. Poets have expressed this very beautifully. T. S. Eliot says:

> *We shall not cease from exploration*
> *and the end of all our exploring*

will be to arrive where we started
and know the place for the first time.

That is Home. Home is where one starts from. This tension of belonging and longing constitutes the dynamism of our inner quest.

Our whole spiritual journey, if I understand it correctly, is set in motion by our longing to go deeper, deeper, and deeper toward that center of our belonging we mean when we say "God." We can identify this movement with a term coined by Christopher Fry, "exploration into God." This is another aspect of the religiousness within religion. We can explore together. We can make discoveries within the realm of divine reality. And tremendous discoveries have been made. Explorers have set up signposts throughout the millennia. These signposts mark insights beyond which one cannot go back.

But there is a question we must ask ourselves: "How does one get from religion to a specific religion?" This is a fascinating question for me: "How does one start out with religiousness and end up with religions?" Are these not opposite poles? Yet, if you bounce it off your own experience, I think you will find it to be true that religiousness inevitably leads to a religion. This may be your own personal religion or a more traditional, established one. In either case, a religion always comprises *doctrine, ethics,* and *ritual.* And these three inevitably develop out of our religiousness, out of our deepest sense of belonging. Inevitably, because our intellect interprets this belonging, and so we get doctrine; our willing commitment to that belonging and to its implications inevitably leads to ethics; and our emotions cannot help celebrating the joy of that belonging, which inevitably creates ritual. Let us look at this process in greater detail.

The moment we become aware of belonging, we cannot help thinking about it. That means interpreting it. And the moment we have interpreted it, even in the most rudimentary way, we have the phenomenon of doctrine. Even in a negative way, if all we say is "this experience cannot be interpreted," that is also an interpretation. We have entered the realm of doctrine.

Doctrine belongs to every religion. But doctrine has a way of becoming *doctrinaire,* as we can immediately see. The more we say, the more we tend to become doctrinaire. Doctrine replaces experience. That is where religion becomes irreligious. But doctrine is originally meant to bring home to you your experience by interpreting it. Doctrine wants to lead to experience. By availing yourself of the interpretations that others have given to the mystical experience through the millennia, you can explore into God, map in hand. And I can assure you it is a great privilege that one can stand in traditions like my own and have its help. It is like having to invent the wheel all over again, or calculus, if you do not have a tradition that helps you understand.

Secondly, our sense of belonging calls for *action.* If you really feel your belonging so profoundly, then you have to act accordingly. You belong to every human being. You belong to all creatures. You belong to the earth. This imposes on you a *responsibility.* And that is the essence of *morality,* of ethics: living out of the religious responsibility that you have incurred by being human, by being aware of your limitless belonging. But now your moral obligations become codified and spelled out in do's and don'ts and soon *morality* becomes *moralistic.* That is another point where religion goes off and becomes more and more irreligious. *Moralism* is irreligious because in the end all these moral codes can prevent you from acting as one acts toward those to whom one belongs.

The third area is *celebration.* Spontaneously, you celebrate your mystical awareness. You cannot help it. Your emotions call for it. Religiousness leads to rituals. As long as ritual springs from a genuine awareness of belonging and cultivates that awareness by celebrating it, all is well. But when only hollow forms remain and the experience is gone, or when the forms even block the experience, then we have no longer ritual, but *ritualism,* an irreligious phenomenon. It is our responsibility to fill the rituals we have inherited with new life or else to allow the wellspring of life that created the old forms to bring forth new ones.

There is no religion that does not have doctrine, morals, and ritual. It must be so, as we have seen. Even for one's private religion, this holds true. For we cannot help it that our intellect, our will, and our emotions, each in its own way, deal with our mystical awareness. Nor, of course, is there anything wrong with doctrine, ethics, and ritual as such except for their tendency to harden into lifeless "isms."

The image I have in mind is that of a volcano. Our mystical experience is like a volcanic eruption. Fire, heat, light gush forth from our innermost depth. But the hot lava flows down the side of the mountain and cools off. The farther we are in space and time from the fiery eruption, the more this glowing magma turns into cold rock. Our task is to push through the "isms" of our particular religion as through thick layers of volcanic rock and to catch fire from the original fire. After all, that is what all the great masters and saints have done. If you stand in an ancient tradition, as I do, there is work to be done. But there are also incredible resources to be tapped if we push through the ossified encrustations.

That's my view of the relationship between religion and the religions. What does it tell us in the context of this conference? What is its relevance for our League for Spiritual Discovery? It tells us that we have an ally in the religious core of every religion, but we may have a real problem with religious institutions—at least until we help them become more genuinely religious than they tend to be. In this effort we have allies in every religious tradition—the truly religious people. They are to be found outside as well as inside any religious institution. It doesn't really matter if that is Buddhism, Hinduism, Christianity in any of its brands, Judaism, or any other religion. They present a problem because they are so paradoxical in themselves. Religions can be channels for religiousness, and they can be dampers that squelch religiousness. It all depends on whether you indulge in them or go through with them—through the rock to the fire.

There are no shortcuts. It has been pointed out with regard to entheogens that they do their thing only if you work with them. That is equally true of religions. If you take a tool of that kind, it has to be used with the grain. That was the main point I wanted to share with you. Maybe some more specific questions on our agenda will take on a different perspective within this frame of reference.

3 *DAS MUTTERKORN:* THE MAKING OF DELYSID

Dale Pendell

Dale Pendell is a poet, a software engineer, and a longtime student of ethnobotany. His poetry has appeared in many journals in the United States and abroad and was anthologized in *Beneath A Single Moon* and in *Dimensions of a Life,* a book about the life and work of Gary Snyder. He was the founding editor of *KUKSU: Journal of Backcountry Writing.* His award-winning, poetical ethnobotanical trilogy, *Pharmako/Poeia, Pharmako/Dynamics,* and *Pharmako/Gnosis* was published by Mercury House. His subsequent books include *The Language of Birds, Inspired Madness, Walking with Nobby,* and *The Great Bay.* Dale leads workshops on botany and ethnopoetics. His blog is http://dalependell.com.

What next? Then the ceremony really began and the initiates apparently went through certain experiences which left them perhaps filled with awe and even confusion, but also overflowing with bliss and joy. What were those experiences? . . . After all, Aristotle specifically stated that

29

the initiates were not going to learn anything, but they
were to suffer, to feel, to experience certain impressions and
psychic moods. . . .

GEORGE MYLONAS, *ELEUSIS AND*
THE ELEUSINIAN MYSTERIES, 1961

1. The Preparation

Albert Hofmann received his doctorate
"with distinction," having cracked the secret
of chitin, which had eluded many others,
in three months, by employing the digestive juices
of a snail, common in vineyards.
He turned down
two high paying offers
in order to work with natural products
at Sandoz.

When the earth opened, Dysaules's son Eubouleus
lost his pigs, but kept
his wits, marked the spot,
so when the Mother came, looking
for her girl, the swineherd
was able to show her
the cave.

I created front companies to buy
fifteen pounds of ergotamine. Tried to make sure
the purchases couldn't be
traced.

Plane trees on the banks of the Ilissos.
Poppies, poppy wine, and a pig-roast,
bloody hands, praying to Demeter.

The goddess
had fasted nine days:
"Initiates into the sea."

2. The Sacred Way

Sprigs of myrtle,
Hofmann studying ergot, sharing a fanless fume hood
with two other chemists, not allowed
any of the company ergotamine, patiently
learning the secrets of the mother corn,
by himself.

We needed six gallons of hydrazine:
you get iso-lysergic hydrazide, but
you can isomerize it later.

On the fifth day,
the mystai
gathered in the morning, left by the Sacred Gate in
the Potters Quarter, began the long walk to Eleusis.
Singing and festivities:
"Come, arise, awaken from your sleep!"

The mushroom trail started in Russia, birch conifer
forests stretching from Estonia
to Kamchatka, the Wassons
tracking the penis of god
across the Caucasus to the Indus River.
Agni and Soma, horsemen, worshippers of the
    Trinity,
they knew birch, beaver, herding, and metallurgy,
the spoked wheel, cannabis, and patrilineal descent.

3. The Bridge

The road dropped from the pass back
to the sea, sparkling blue and aquamarine
like a plate of cut gems: Phryne
stripped, in front of everybody,
let her hair down and waded in:
inspired Apelles's painting
"Aphrodite
rising from the sea."

Do the reaction under nitrogen. We chained two acid
      traps on the end to catch the vapors. Pre-heat the
      oil bath.
We did 250 grams at a time. The reaction takes an hour.
Rotovac the hydrazide. Rinse the flask and vacuum
      distill
with an iced condenser.

The river dry now, hard to find,
cement factories, tall smokestacks
steaming, the marble pillars
of the Telesterion still lying
in the fields past the chain link fence—
smoke where incense was, dust on dust:
a cloud over Eleusis.

LSD had been created and abandoned, Hofmann
      seeking a cure
for migraine headache;
pharmacology, working with mice,
had noted only "a certain restlessness"
and thought the drug not worth pursuing.
Five years later Hofmann had "a peculiar
      presentiment"

that something in recipe 25
had been missed.

In Chicago
the reactor went critical.

They offered wine to the grieving goddess,
she refused, instead requested
a mixed potion of water and white barley,
fresh leaves of glechon—
Mentha pulegium: pennyroyal.

Robert Graves
sent a note to Wasson
that a mushroom cult
might still exist
in Mexico, in the highlands
of Oaxaca. Wasson
funded the expedition
himself. The CIA
planted a mole.

Dissolve the hydrazide in tartaric acid, basify, and
    extract
with chloroform until you can't see any more lysergic
in the solvent with uv long. Dry the chloroform
and rotovac. Store the lysergic hydrazide
in the refrigerator under nitrogen.

Iambe raised her skirt and flashed her butt;
she swirled her hips around and pumped—
no one could cross the bridge without some rude
licentious joke or gesture: men felt up and derided,

the women goosed. Sex
in the air like a mist.
We laughed and sang:
"Iakchos! Iakchos!"

4. The Dance

Hofmann
set about synthesizing
a few centigrams of lysergic acid diethylamide.
He was careful, but had to abandon the
    recrystallization
of the tartrate salt when his mind was oddly
stimulated. He went home, lay down, closed his eyes,
saw the universe swirl, wondered what could be the
    cause.
Next day tried inhaling each of the solvents
he had used, then determined
to try a self-experiment, figured, back of the
    envelope,
what would be one-tenth
of a minimal dose, based on what he knew of ergot
alkaloids, took 250 micrograms of LSD 25
on the 19th of April, 1943.

The mystai passed the rock where
the goddess had rested, where, weeping,
she had stopped at the Virgin's Well
and met the inhabitants of Eleusis.
She sat on a white sheepskin.

Whirling woman, woman of colors,
Woman of network of light

I am a shooting star woman, says
I am a music woman, says

After two days on foot, by horse and mule, Wasson
reached Huatla. Mentioned the name
ʔnti¹xi³tho³
to the constable, who stared at him a long time.

That night everyone danced:
girls played pipes, tambourines;
we held torches. The women
danced with the sacred cup
balanced on their heads.

In complete darkness, or dim red light under nitrogen
convert the hydrazide to pyrazole
with pentanedione. Neutralize
with sodium hydroxide and refrigerate the flask
to precipitate the crystals.
Vacuum dry for twelve hours.

On the night September 27th, 480 B.C.E.,
two Greek renegades, traveling with Xerxes,
reported that,
their countrymen all in flight, the Mysteries
were nonetheless performed, that they had seen
the white light break forth
from the Anaktoron; that the gods
had performed what men could not.

Do the aminization in red light under nitrogen.
Dry the diethylamine just before you use it.
Heat on an oil bath for four hours.

You need high vacuum. Potassium hydroxide
in methanol converts
the "iso" to "d."

Late at night, we entered
the sanctuary. The priestesses
came in with the kykeon,
a measured portion
for each to drink.

5. The Light

Hofmann realized that his world was dissolving—left
    Sandoz
and rode home four kilometers
on his bicycle. Thought he might be dying, had his
    assistant
call his doctor, who, though puzzled, assured him
that all of his vital signs were normal.
After that he relaxed. Was moved
by a truth so simple, so obvious,
that the colors, tastes, the flowing sound and stars,
were only glitter.

"I have drunk the mixed potion"

We cleaned all the glassware as best we could,
then broke it all up;
took the pieces to the dump—couldn't risk
that some innocent might try
to use a piece of it
for a vase or something.

Alcibiades got busted, serving up the mysteries
socially, at a party at his home:
a capital crime that the Athenians,
needing his military skills, could never
carry out.

Hofmann succeeded easily
where the CIA had failed,
isolated the magic of the mushrooms
and in an act of shamanic
propriety, made the long journey
to Huatla, to present his molecules
to Maria Sabina.

The goddess gave her secrets
to Triptolemos, and he planted
the world's first grain
in the Rarian fields
below Eleusis, where
steel cranes and oil tankers
crowd the harbor at Salamis.

It took twenty batches. We should have done
it in steps, converted all of the ergotamine to
lysergic hydrazide first, then converted all of the
hydrazide to pyrazole, and then just had the
aminization to do at the end, but once we had
that first batch of hydrazide, we wanted to take it
all the way, to see if the process was going to work.

That was really a mistake, because then we had a
hundred grams of LSD, and as careful as we
could be it got into the air, or the glass, or

somewhere, we never figured out. It took two
more weeks to do the rest. We made two kilos.
We were high the whole time.

After two thousand years
Alaric, hoards of cavalry, miles of dust,
crossed through the pass at Thermopylae
with Christian priests.
The Classical World was closing.

At fragrant Eleusis
the bright light was finally dimmed.

From halfway around the world, Wasson sent
    Hofmann
the seeds of sacred morning glory,
ololiuhqui—the Aztec sacrament—
its identity ferreted out from the Indians,
by priests, with torture.

Albert, analyzing, amazed, found the seeds
contained the same alkaloid already
in his laboratory: lysergic acid amide.
The Mother Grain, Tollkorn, die Taumelloch:

The magic circle
was complete.

Whoever in this world has seen these Mysteries, is
    blessed.

4 THE MESSAGE OF THE ELEUSINIAN MYSTERIES FOR TODAY'S WORLD

Albert Hofmann

Albert Hofmann, Ph.D., Dr.Pharm.H.C., Dr.Sc.Nat.H.C., is best known for his serendipitous discovery of LSD and for his chemical work identifying the active principles of the sacred mushroom of Mexico. He was the retired director of research for the Department of Natural Products at Sandoz Pharmaceutical Ltd. in Basel, Switzerland. Dr. Hofmann was a fellow of the World Academy of Science and a member of the Nobel Prize Committee, the International Society of Plant Research, and the American Society of Pharmacognosy. He wrote many scientific papers and several books: *The Botany and Chemistry of Hallucinogens* and *Plants of the Gods* with Richard Evans Schultes, *The Road to Eleusis* with R. G. Wasson and Carl Ruck, *LSD: My Problem Child,* and *Insight/Outlook.*

Born January 11, 1906, Albert celebrated his 100th birthday in excellent health with thousands of grateful admirers at the Spirit of Basel—a celebration of his life's work (www.lsd.info/en/home.html). Albert died two years later, on

April 29, 2008, four months after his wife, Anita, had passed away. His archives and legacy are managed by Dieter Hagenbach at www.gaiamedia.org.

If our classical scholars were given the opportunity to attend the rite at Eleusis, to talk with the Priestess, what would they not exchange for that chance? . . . How propitious would their frame of mind be, if they were invited to partake of the potion!

R. G. Wasson, "The Hallucinogenic Fungi of Mexico: An Inquiry into the Origins of the Religious Idea among Primitive Peoples," 1961

Whoever among men who walk the Earth has seen these Mysteries is blessed, but whoever is uninitiated and has not received his share of the rite, he will not have the same lot as the others, once he is dead and dwells in the mould where the sun goes down.

THUS READS THE praise in an epic poem known as "The Homeric Hymn to Demeter." The Mysteries referred to here are those of Eleusis, the most important mysteries of Greek antiquity. For almost two thousand years, from around 1500 B.C.E. to the fourth century C.E., these were celebrated at Eleusis, Greece, in honor of the goddess Demeter and her daughter Persephone.

The events leading to the founding of the shrine of Eleusis are described in this Homeric Hymn. The author of this hymn, and his provenience, are unknown, but it must have originated around the end of the seventh century B.C.E.

One day, while Persephone, daughter of Zeus and Demeter, was picking flowers in the lovely meadows, she was abducted by Hades, god of the underworld. Her mother searched for her in vain, finally learning from Helios of the abduction of her daughter. Sorely afflicted, Demeter became alienated from Olympus, since she even came to know that her husband, Zeus, had been in agreement with the kidnapping.

Dressed as a simple woman among humankind, Demeter found friendly abode in the palace of the king of Eleusis, Keleos, and his wife, Metaneira. In gratitude for their friendly hospitality, Demeter founded a temple in Eleusis after revealing herself to be a goddess. To castigate the Olympian gods for the abduction of her daughter, Demeter caused all of the vegetation on Earth to die, threatening humankind with extinction. The gods feared the loss of the prayers and sacrifices of humanity and begged Demeter to make Earth fruitful again. This plea was not granted until Zeus ordered his brother Hades in the underworld to return Persephone to her mother. Mother and daughter returned to Olympus, but henceforth Persephone had to spend a third of the year with her spouse in the underworld. When she did, winter reigned on Earth. Yet every year, when Persephone returned to Earth in the spring, the plant world awoke anew with flowers and bore fruits.

Before Demeter returned to the other gods on Olympus, she instructed the kings of Eleusis, Keleos and Triptolemus, how to celebrate the rites in her temple. These were secret precepts, Mysteries to be closely guarded. Divulging or profaning them was punishable by death. In appreciation of the propitious outcome of the drama of Eleusis, Demeter bestowed upon Triptolemus, the first initiate of Eleusis, a sprig of grain and bade him instruct humankind in agriculture.

The cult of Demeter and Persephone in Eleusis, which was initially of only local significance, soon became an important part of Athenian citizenship, and it eventually developed into a pan-Hellenic institution, becoming of universal importance at the time of the Roman empire. Its character as a pan-Hellenic institution was signaled in 760 B.C.E., at the time of the fifth Olympiad, when the Oracle of Delphi called upon all Greeks to make communal sacrifice in honor of Demeter of Eleusis in order to banish a famine that was then affecting all of Greece.

What was the message conveyed at Eleusis, a message that

transformed the cult into the most influential and spiritually significant Mystery of antiquity? This question cannot be answered in detail, for the veil of mystery, maintained by a severe commandment of secrecy, was never lifted during the millennia. It is only by examining the testimony of great initiates that we may gain an idea of the fundamentals and the spiritual significance that the teachings of Eleusis had for the individual. There is no question of any new religion having been promulgated in Eleusis; this can be ruled out because the initiates, when they returned to their homelands after the Mysteries, remained faithful to their autochthonous religions.

Instead, revelations about the essence of human existence and about the meaning of life and death must have been imparted to the initiates. Prayers are known from the Mysteries, offered by initiates to Mnemosyne, the goddess of memory, imploring her to awaken and vividly maintain the memory of the holy initiation, that the initiation might persist as an experience illuminating all of life and transforming existence.

Participating in the Mysteries was an experience that cannot be understood by examining only their external appearance, for it evoked alterations in the soul of the initiate. This is evident from the testimony of the most famous initiates. Thus wrote Pindar of the Eleusinian blessing:

> *Blessed is he who, having seen these rites,*
> *undertakes the way beneath the Earth.*
> *He knows the end of life,*
> *as well as its divinely granted beginning.*

Cicero also attested to the splendor that illuminated his life from Eleusis:

> *Not only have we found there the reason to live more joyously, but also*
> *that we may die with greater hope.*

The initiates often experienced in vision the congruity of the beginning and the end, of birth and death, the totality and the eternal generative ground of being. It must have been an encounter with the ineffable, an encounter with the divine, that could only be described through metaphor. It is striking that the Eleusinian experience is described again and again in antitheses: darkness and light, terror and beatitude. This ambivalence is also evident in other descriptions, such as that of Aelius Aristides, who stated that Eleusis was:

> *Both the most awesome and the most luminous*
> *of all the divine things that exist among men.*

Emperor Marcus Aurelius counted the Mysteries among those endowments that manifest the solicitude of the gods for humankind.

We know as little of the essence of the ritual by which the illuminating vision was transmitted to the initiates as we know of the meaning of the vision itself. The events leading up to the inner sanctum, to the *telesterion,* in which the crux of the Mystery took place, are amply documented. The preparatory, so-called Lesser Mysteries were celebrated in Athens in springtime, in the month of flowers, *Anthesterion.* The celebration of the Greater Mysteries began annually in Athens in autumn, in the month *Boedromion,* which today corresponds to the end of September and beginning of October. After four days of rites and festivities in the city, the solemn procession to Eleusis, some fourteen miles distant, began with great pomp on the fifth day.

During the procession, rites, sacrifices, and purification ceremonies took place publicly, and these have therefore been made known to us in full detail. On the sixth day, sacrifices, festivities, and purification rites took place in Eleusis on the outskirts of the sanctuary. These have also been amply described. What then took place that night at the climax of the Eleusinian ceremony, in the inner sanctum of the temple, the telesterion, into which only the priests and the initiates could enter, has in essence remained a mystery. The law of secrecy was forever maintained.

What we do know, and what is crucial in the present context, is that before the climax of the initiation, before the illuminating vision of the initiates, a sacred potion, the *kykeon,* was administered. We also know that the kykeon was composed of barley and mint. In recent times, scholars of Eleusis have advanced the hypothesis that the kykeon must have contained some hallucinogenic compound. This would explain how it was possible for the priests to simultaneously induce, as if in programmed fashion, an ecstatic-visionary state in hundreds of initiates.

Thus, the problem of the kykeon is an essential part of the secrets of Eleusis. Could the visions of Eleusis have been produced solely by unknown rites, or was the kykeon a *psychopharmakon,* a plant extract capable of inducing an ecstatic state?

This question also brings us to a problem of our own time. This involves the question—much discussed today—of whether it is ethically and religiously defensible to use consciousness-altering drugs under specific circumstances to gain new insights into the spiritual world.

But before we consider this question, let us return to the problem of the kykeon. If the potion did indeed contain an hallucinogenic compound, then what sort of hallucinogen might it have been? This question is still relevant. Two scholars of the Mysteries have considered it: first, Professor Karl Kerenyi, who published two books about the Mysteries, and then ethnomycologist R. Gordon Wasson, who approached me for assistance because I had become an expert on the chemical aspects of the problem following my discovery of the highly active hallucinogen LSD and my research into the Mexican magic plants.

The investigation regarding the putative hallucinogen of the kykeon that I conducted in collaboration with Gordon Wasson and Carl Ruck, professor of ethnobotany in Greek mythology at Boston University, uncovered interesting parallels and connections between the Eleusinian Mystery cult and certain extant magic cults among the Indian tribes in remote regions of southern Mexico.

In the Mazatec and Zapotec regions of the mountains of southern Mexico, the thaumaturges and *curanderos* continue, as they have for millennia, to employ an hallucinogenic potion in their magico-religious curing ceremonies. This potion is prepared from the seeds of certain species of morning glories, *Turbina corymbosa* and *Ipomoea violacea*. In the chemical-pharmaceutical research laboratories of Sandoz Ltd. in Basel, Switzerland, we have investigated the active principles of this drug, known as the *ololiuhqui* potion. These proved to be alkaloids also found in ergot, namely *lysergic acid amide* and *lysergic acid hydroxyethyl-amide,* near relatives of *lysergic acid diethylamide,* the chemical name for LSD, also a product of ergot.

We also found the very same hallucinogenic compounds in ergot of the wild grass *Paspalum distichum* from the Mediterranean area. These findings led us to frame the hypothesis that the consciousness-altering component of the kykeon involved hallucinogenic compounds similar to those used to this day in the preparation of the sacred ololiuhqui potion. The Eleusinian priests merely had to collect the ergot of this *Paspalum* species, which surely was very common in the vicinity of the temple, and then pulverize it and add it to the kykeon to give it its consciousness-altering potency.

Ergot is the name of the sclerotium of the lower fungus *Claviceps,* which parasitizes grains and also wild grasses like *Paspalum*. The ears of grain infested by the fungus form dark pegs in place of the normally light-colored grains—this is ergot. It is not at all unlikely that ergot would have been used as a sacred drug in the temple of the goddess of grain, Demeter.

A further connection between ergot and Eleusis is shown in an Eleusinian ritual that consisted of the presentation of an ear of grain by the priests. This ritual is related to the myth of the barleycorn, which dies planted in the earth in order to give life to a new plant that leaps forth again to the light of springtime. Here we find a symbol of the annual rotation of Persephone from the darkness of the underworld to the light of Olympus, as well as a symbol of the permanence of life in the eternal cycle of death and rebirth.

The studies leading to the hypothesis of an ergot preparation as the

Eleusinian drug were published in a 1978 book by Wasson, Hofmann, and Ruck, *The Road to Eleusis*.* If the hypothesis that an LSD-like consciousness-altering drug was present in the kykeon is correct—and there are good arguments in its favor—then the Eleusinian Mysteries have a relevance for our time in not only a spiritual-existential sense, but also with respect to the question of the controversial use of consciousness-altering compounds to attain mystical insights into the riddle of life.

In the second part of this paper, I will be concerned with the following two questions:

1. What was the historic-spiritual function of the Eleusinian Mysteries in Greek antiquity?
2. Why and to what extent can the Mysteries serve as a model for our time?

The great importance and long duration of the Mysteries indicate that they answered a profound spiritual necessity, a yearning of the soul. If we adopt the viewpoint of Nietzsche, the Greek spirit was characterized by a divided consciousness of reality from its origin. Greece was the cradle of an experience of reality in which the ego felt itself separated from the exterior world. Here, conscious separation of the individual from the environment developed earlier than in other cultures. This dualistic worldview, which the German physician and writer Gottfried Benn has characterized as the *European destiny neurosis,* has figured decisively in the course of European spiritual history, and is still fully operative in the Western world.

An ego that is capable of confronting the exterior world and regarding the world objectively as matter—a spirit capable of objectivizing the external world—was a precondition for the appearance of Western scientific research. This objective worldview is evident in even the earliest documents of scientific thought, in the cosmologi-

---

*The Road to Eleusis, New York: Harcourt Brace Jovanich. [A thirtieth anniversary edition of this book was published by North Atlantic Books in 2008. —Ed.]

cal theories of the Greek pre-Socratic philosophers. The perspective of man in opposition to nature, which has made possible a vigorous domination of nature, was given its first clear philosophical formulation by Descartes in the seventeenth century. Thus, in Europe, a wholly objective, quantitative scientific investigation of nature has developed that has made it possible to explain the physical and chemical laws of the composition of the material world. Its findings also made possible a hitherto nonexistent exploitation of nature and her forces. It has led to the industrialization and mechanization of nearly all aspects of modern life. It has brought a small portion of humankind a level of comfort and material well-being hitherto scarcely imaginable. It has also resulted in the catastrophic destruction of the natural environment, and now has produced a global ecological crisis.

Even more serious than the material consequences is the spiritual damage of this evolution, which has led to a materialistic worldview. The individual has lost the connection with the spiritual, divine ground of all being. Unprotected, without shelter, and alone with oneself, the human individual confronts in solitude a soulless, chaotic, materialistic, and menacing universe. The seeds of this dualistic worldview, which has manifested itself so catastrophically in our time, were, as previously mentioned, already evident in Greek antiquity. The Greek genius sought the cure, so that the external, material world, under Apollo's protection, could be seen in its sublime beauty. The colorful, joyous, sensual, but also painful Apollonian world was complemented by the Dionysian world of experience, in which the subject/object cleavage was dissolved in ecstatic inebriation.

Nietzsche wrote of the Dionysian worldview in *The Birth of Tragedy*.

It is either through the influence of narcotic potions, of which all primitive peoples and races speak in hymns, or through the powerful approach of spring, penetrating all of nature with joy, that those Dionysian stirrings arise, which in their intensification lead

the individual to forget himself completely. . . . Not only does the
bond between person and person come to be forged once again by
the magic of the Dionysian rite, but alienated, hostile, or subjugated
nature again celebrates her reconciliation with her prodigal son,
mankind.

The Eleusinian Mysteries were closely connected with the rites
and festivities in honor of the god Dionysus. They led essentially to
healing, to the transcendence of the division between humankind
and nature—one might say to the abolition of the separation between
creator and creation. This was the real, greater proposition of the
Eleusinian Mysteries. Their historical, cultural significance, their
influence on European spiritual history, can scarcely be overestimated.
Here, suffering humanity, split by its rational, objective spirit, found
healing in a mystical experience of totality that made it possible for
the individual to believe in the immortality of an eternal being.

This belief persisted in early Christianity, albeit with different
symbols. It is found as a promise in certain passages of the Gospels,
most clearly in the Gospel of John 14:16–20. There, Jesus addresses
his disciples as he takes leave of them:

> And I will pray the Father,
> and He shall give you another comforter,
> that He may abide with you forever in the Truth. . . .
> At that day ye shall know that I am the Father,
> and ye in me, and I in you.

But ecclesiastical Christianity, defined by the duality of cre-
ator/creation and with a religiosity estranged from nature, has completely obliterated the Eleusinian-Dionysian heritage of antiquity. In
the Christian sphere of belief, only specially blessed people testify
to a timeless, comforting reality attained in spontaneous visionary
experience—an experience that untold numbers of people could attain

in antiquity through the Eleusinian initiation. The *unio mystica* of the Catholic saints and the visionary ecstasy described in the writings of Jakob Boehme, Meister Eckhart, Angelius Silesius, Teresa von Avila, Juan de la Cruz, Thomas Traherne, William Blake, and others are obviously closely related to the "enlightenment" attained by the initiates to the Eleusinian Mysteries.

Today the fundamental importance that a mystical experience of totality can have for healing a humanity afflicted by a one-sided, rational, materialistic worldview is emphasized not only by adherents to Eastern religious currents such as Zen Buddhism, but also by leading representatives of psychology and psychiatry. Even more significant is that not just in medicine, but in ever-wider circles of our society, even ecclesiastical circles, overcoming the dualistic worldview is considered to be a prerequisite and fundamental step in the healing and spiritual renewal of Occidental civilization and culture.

The official Christian churches, whose dogmas correspond to an expressly dualistic conception of the world, offer little room for such a renewal. Rather, it is private groups and associations who are attempting to satisfy the need and the longing for an all-encompassing experience of the world appropriate to our present level of knowledge and consciousness. Great numbers of all sorts of workshops and courses in yoga, meditation, and self-encounter are being offered, all with the goal of an alteration or expansion of consciousness. A new direction, transpersonal psychology, has branched off from academic psychiatry and psychology, which are based on a dualistic conception of reality. In this new discipline, various means are sought to aid the individual to attain a healing experience of totality. More and more, individuals seek security and shelter through meditation, pressing onward into deeper levels of experience of reality.

It is no accident that drugs are employed by these groups and in the private sphere as pharmacological aids in the production of altered states of consciousness. And, of course, this involves the same sort of drugs hypothesized at Eleusis and still used by certain Indian tribes.

These are the *psychopharmaka* of the hallucinogenic class, which have also been described as *psychedelics* or *entheogens,* whose most important modern representative is LSD. The Greeks used the term *pharmacotheon,* or "divine drug." This sort of psychotropic compound differs from the opiates, such as morphine and heroin, and from such stimulants as cocaine, in that they do not produce addiction and act specifically on human consciousness.

LSD in particular played an important role in the '60s movement, which addressed war and materialism, and whose adherents sought to expand consciousness. As a matter of fact, under specific internal and external conditions, this class of drugs, whether called hallucinogens, psychedelics, or entheogens, is capable of producing a totality experience, the unio mystica. Before the use of these substances was prohibited worldwide, this effect was applied in academic psychiatry to assist psychoanalytic and psychotherapeutic treatment from the pharmacological side.

A prerequisite for meaningful use and a propitious psychic experience of these compounds—which can be described as sacred drugs—is the external environment and the spiritual preparation of those experimenting with them. The Mexican Indians believe that were the LSD-like ololiuhqui taken by an impure person, that is, anybody who was not prepared for the ceremony with fasts and prayers, then the drug might provoke insanity or even death. This wise and prudent manner of use, based on millennia of experience, was regrettably not heeded when many members of our society began to use psychedelics. Accordingly, the results sometimes took the form of psychotic breakdowns and severe accidents. In the 1960s, this led to the prohibition of any use of this type of drug, even in formal psychiatry.

In Eleusis, where the preparations and the associated ceremonies were optimal (as is still the case among some Indian groups in Mexico where their use is still in the control of shamans), this sort of drug found a meaningful and propitious application. From this perspective, Eleusis and these Indian groups can indeed serve as a model for our society.

In conclusion, I wish once more to raise the fundamental question, Why were such drugs probably used in Eleusis, and why are they still used by certain Indian tribes even today in the course of religious ceremonies? And why is such use scarcely conceivable in the Christian liturgy, as though it were not significant? The answer is that the Christian liturgy worships a godly power enthroned in heaven, that is, a power outside of the individual. At Eleusis, on the contrary, an alteration in the innermost being of the individual was striven for, a visionary experience of the ground of being that converted the subjects into mystes, epotetes, initiates.

Alteration within the individual is again under way today. The requisite transformations in the direction of an all-encompassing consciousness, as a precondition for overcoming materialism and for a renewed relationship with nature, cannot be relegated to society or to the state. The change must and can only take place in each individual person.

Only a few blessed people spontaneously attain the mystical vision that can effect this transformation. As a result, mankind has repeatedly sought paths and evolved methods to evoke deeper perception and experience. First among these are the different techniques of meditation. Meditation can be assisted by such external means as isolation and solitude, a path the hermits and desert saints followed, and by such physical practices as fasting and breath control. An especially important aid in the induction of mystical-ecstatic states of consciousness, discovered in the earliest times, is decidedly the use of certain plant drugs. In the preceding discussion, I have made it quite clear that their use must proceed within the scope of religious ceremony.

The fact that extraordinary states of awareness can be induced with various means and in various ways shows us that capacity for mystical experience is innate to every person. It is part of the essence of human spirituality. It is unrelated to the external, social status of the individual. Thus, in Eleusis, free men and women, as well as slaves, could be initiated.

Eleusis can be a model for today. Eleusis-like centers could unite and strengthen the many spiritual currents of our time, all of which have the same goal: the goal of creating, by transforming consciousness in individual people, the conditions for a better world, a world without war and without environmental damage, a world of happy people.

5 A NEW VOCABULARY
Ann and Alexander Shulgin

Ann Shulgin was born in Wellington, New Zealand, in 1931, the daughter of the American consul. She lived in various countries with her family before settling in northern California. She has written papers on psychotherapy with MDMA and, with her husband, a protocol for the evaluation of new psychoactive drugs. With David Nichols and her husband, Alexander, she coauthored the novel, *PIHKAL: A Chemical Love Story* and then went on to pen a second novel with Alexander titled *TIHKAL: A Continuation,* which was published in 1997.

Alexander Shulgin took his Ph.D. in biochemistry from the University of California, Berkeley, in 1954 after attending Harvard and serving in the U.S. Navy. He became a research chemist and scientific consultant for industrial, educational, and government organizations including Dow Chemical, the National Institute on Drug Abuse, Lawrence Radiation Laboratory, Drug Enforcement Administration, Bristol Laboratories, and others. Dr. Shulgin has written approximately two hundred scientific papers and holds twenty patents for his research in various disciplines. He has lectured at the University of California, Berkeley, the Pacific Graduate School of Psychology, and San Francisco State University.

[We are] entering upon a discussion where the vocabulary of the English language is seriously deficient. There are no apt words in them to characterize your state when you are, shall we say, "bemushroomed." We are all, willy nilly, confined within the prison walls of our everyday vocabulary. With skill in our choice of words we may stretch accepted meanings to cover slightly new feelings and thoughts, but when a state of mind is utterly distinct, wholly novel, then all our old words fail. How do you tell a man born blind what seeing is like? . . . How curious it is that modern civilized man finds surcease from care in a drug for which he seems to have no respect! If we use by analogy the terms suitable for alcohol, we prejudice the mushroom, and since there are few among us who have been bemushroomed, there is danger that the experience will not be fairly judged. What we need is a vocabulary to describe all the modalities of the Divine Inebriant. . . .

R. G. WASSON, "THE HALLUCINOGENIC FUNGI OF
MEXICO: AN INQUIRY INTO THE ORIGINS OF THE
RELIGIOUS IDEA AMONG PRIMITIVE PEOPLES," 1961

This paper is based on a presentation made at the twenty-second Annual Conference of the Association for Humanistic Psychology on August 21–26, 1984, in Boston, Massachusetts, and is an abridged version of a chapter in the Shulgins' book, TIHKAL: A Continuation.

SEVERAL YEARS AGO, at a symposium in Santa Barbara, California, an audience gathered to hear about and discuss "entheogens," a word created to mean "generation of God within"—yet another name for psychoactive drugs. Our presentation there was an answer to an often-asked question, "Why do you do the work that you do?" What are our reasons for the designing, the making, and the evaluation of drugs that can bring a person into some form of understanding of the drives and unconscious motivations of himself and other people? And why the subsequent publication of this work and its results?

We had named a number of substances that had been developed— some by ourselves and some by others—which we chose to refer to by words in the vocabulary of communication, words that allow the exchanges of understanding and insights. We had felt that the chemicals were the words of vocabulary; we feel now that this concept is not correct. The vocabulary is not composed of the catalysts that evoke the experiences; the vocabulary is created by the experiences themselves.

What we are doing is looking, as have countless others before us, for a way to communicate the experiences of the deeper parts of ourselves, a way to share knowledge that has traditionally been called "occult," or "hidden," and that has been, until our time, considered the private preserve of those few shamans, teachers, or spiritual guides in each culture who had earned their way to it.

In their hands was the responsibility of choosing from the multitude the gifted, intuitive people who would become students or disciples. These special ones were taken into temples of learning, into the pyramids, the secret lodges, the monasteries, or the sacred kivas, and were slowly led into a recognition of their own interior landscape. These guided explorations evolved, in time, into a state of mind and heart that was then—and still is now—known as wisdom.

We now live in a time when these teachings are completely in the open. They are exposed and available, in books, on tapes, on television and radio, in magazines and newspapers, by letter or telephone—a thousand and one places. Secrecy is no longer necessary in this Western culture filled with noise, both auditory and visual, and those who are not prepared to hear or see, learn nothing. In our present-day Western world, true secrecy is often—if not always—a tool of power seekers, of men and women who know the attraction of the forbidden and mysterious to the naive person who is willing to be controlled and led.

We are here today to try to explain why we feel it essential to attempt to instill a greater awareness, an expansion of conscious knowing, in the people who lead our society and shape its direction. We can no longer trust to time, as our ancestors did, to the gradual and natural unfolding and evolution of comprehension and wisdom.

We do not think we have the time.

If we did have the time that our ancestors had, we would expect to see a gradual increase in the number of people aware of the interior workings, the energies, the complex balancing of drives, fears, instincts, and learned patterns, which make up the interior universe of the human being. We would have reason to anticipate an eventual growth in understanding of the nature of mind, soul, and psyche. Until recently, this growth had been keeping pace with, and counterbalancing, the flowering of knowledge in the physical world. In the last few decades, developments in physics, chemistry, electronics, mathematics, and information distribution have occurred at a rate unique in human history. The impact on even the most intelligent and thoughtful people in our Western world has been so massive, and so rapid, as to have produced a state of mind known now as "future shock."

This understanding of the nature of the physical world has not, however, had the necessary and vital counterpart in the understanding of the nature of the human unconscious, of the images and emotions and energies that determine the uses to which the knowledge of physical matter may be directed.

We see all around us the results of unconscious projection, unconscious archetypal energies, and this time, instead of having reason to fear the destruction of a culture, or a race, or a civilization, we are facing the complete annihilation of the form of life known as mankind, a final end to the entire human experiment. What we do not acknowledge consciously, and what we have not allowed ourselves to confront consciously, may this time kill all of us.

The concept of "archetypes" was made familiar to us by Carl Jung. One can also describe them as fundamental psychic energies presenting themselves within the human psyche as powerful images. The Jungian analyst John Perry has given a good definition of what is meant by archetypes. "They are," he says, "components of the deeper layer of the psyche which express themselves in mythic or symbolic imagery, and which portray the developmental process of the individual—and the culture. The archetype is made of image and emotion; the image presents the meaning of the emotion, and the emotion gives the image its dynamic energy. It is autonomous, usually residing in the unconscious. In order for the archetype to be experienced consciously, it is necessary for the individual to be in an altered state of consciousness, however induced."

Until we are prepared to undertake that most essential of all explorations, the difficult but rewarding journey of discovery into our inner universe, we will continue to make choices motivated by the unseen, unrecognized, and unadmitted energies and images within us, both constructive and destructive.

Our political leaders will continue to make decisions based on the energies engendered mostly by the destructive archetypes and those of power and control. The difference between our present time and any earlier time in history is that, among the tools available to unconsciously motivated leaders, there are now brand-new ones known as nuclear weapons.

Most of the great religions and spiritual belief systems of the world have chosen to deal with archetypes in projection, as aspects of the spiritual world with which humans must deal in order to survive. In the mythologies of all cultures we find ways of portraying the duality of life-giving and death-dealing, of nurturing and destroying.

It is easy to believe that the most insightful and spiritually advanced wise men of each culture must have realized that these forces of light and dark lived within their own psyches. It is also reasonable to assume that the priest-kings of ancient times gained and kept power by externalizing these archetypal images as gods and demons, and by assuring the people over whom they ruled that only they, themselves, knew how to keep these entities satisfied and thus benign.

In Greece, for example, the gods and goddesses of Mount Olympus mirrored the contradictory nature of man. For each Demeter, representing life and growth, there was a Hades who brought cold and death and who had to be granted his time and his due. And usually, within each god and goddess there were two aspects—the giving, teaching, and nurturing aspect, and the revengeful and destructive aspect. In teaching the people by means of stories and ceremonial rituals, the priests acquainted them with the means of handling these various human impulses and contradictions. They were not known as the "destructive instinct," the "nurturing and connecting impulse," the "power drive," but as Zeus and Athena and Aphrodite, Hermes and Hestia. Those who chose to pay attention to the lessons contained in the stories, honoring the needs of these projected energies by means of ceremony and sacrifice, were expected to live lives of relative safety and contentment.

Every culture has had such god-images, and throughout thousands of years the archetypes that, in reality, reside within us have been given names and places outside us—on the sacred mountaintop, above the altar, beneath the earth where the dead ancestors dwell, inside the secret cave, or at the bottom of the sea. Buddha and Ahriman, Christ and Satan, Lucifer and Shiva, Kwan-Yin (the Chinese goddess of mercy and compassion) and the Black Kali (the Indian goddess of blood and death)—all are outside. Their existence inside us has remained unacknowledged by the conscious mind.

In a day when a majority of the public in this country is increasingly well-informed and has some exposure to logical thinking, the ancient god-forms of these interior energies are less often mentioned; rather, our projections are made onto other cultures, other ways of life and thinking. Satan may not be popular, but the Soviet Union, for many years, took its place satisfactorily. In modern-day Iraq and Iran, America is the new devil, the convenient embodiment of the terrible, evil "other."

It has been the habit of people in positions of power and influence, both in the past and in our own time, to discourage individual, unguided, and undirected exploration into the interior of the human psyche. The reasons given for such discouragement are many, and often based on realistic concerns. Among the more altruistic reasons given for limiting the means and forms of self-discovery is one that bears the stamp of truth: that this kind of exploration may well be accompanied by emotional shock and an overturning of long-held and deeply cherished beliefs. We, too, believe that it should be attempted only by a person who has succeeded in developing a strong central core, a sense of self—someone who has had the conscious experience of the awareness of himself as being, and with it, the awareness of the fact that he is aware of being.

This has also been called the "I am" experience and was perhaps best described by the author C. S. Lewis in a small, extraordinary autobiographical work titled *Surprised by Joy*. Only such a person is equipped, according to this argument, to enter the uncharted land of his unconscious self and confront, with expectation of emerging mentally and emotionally whole, the archetypes—both personal and universal—that he will meet.

They are not all dragons. Many of these energies and images are radiant and totally seductive, and it does indeed take practice and a certain degree of emotional and psychological maturity, as well as a strong center, to distinguish between equally luminous and inviting paths, to sense where and when one should go and where and when one should stay and reflect. In the mental health field, for instance, this concern is expressed in the statement that there are many people who cannot and should not undertake the self-exploration known as psychoanalysis.

All around us, we have seen the results of unprepared and unguided self-exploration. There have been unexpected eruptions of the unconscious energies in people whose inner core or sense of self was not sufficiently developed to enable them to structure, control, or gain understanding of the surge of imagery and force from the hidden side of themselves. Most of these people, in the past—as now—spent much of their lives, after such an eruption, in places of confinement of some kind. In modern times, these places are called mental hospitals. On some past occasions, they were put to death as witches; in a few cases they lost themselves in the radiant and loving archetypes and spent their lives as saints or mystics, often just as unable to care for their own daily needs as were the demon-possessed.

These encounters with the interior world have given fuel to the argument that such knowledge is dangerous and that those people who have insisted on exploring these unknown areas—especially if they did so openly—were to be regarded as threatening the peace and safety of their society. This view has merit. However, there is another side to the argument.

Societies are usually led by people whose focus and energy are fueled by the power drive—what can perhaps be called the power archetype. It is an aspect of the self that all explorers of the psyche will meet, sooner or later.

The power aspect is able to make decisions and to formulate rules and systems; it structures and it drives to control. Without it, mankind would have perished long ago. The power drive shapes our world. Kept in balance with its several complementary energies, it gives us form; it builds civilizations.

But when the precarious balance is shifted and too much energy flows from the power drive, structure becomes constriction, control becomes dictatorship, teaching becomes admonition and threat, vision and intuition become dogma, and caution turns into paranoia. Communication with the loving and nurturing energy has been lost, and with it the ability to choose wisely.

When the power aspect is threatened or frustrated and if it remains unconscious, it tends to ally itself with the destructive energy, the part of our human psyche that relates to its surroundings with a drive to contain, incorporate, devour, and kill. It becomes, unconsciously and instinctively, the enemy of its creative counterpart, which is characterized by adaptability, communication, empathy, and transformation. Thus, the implications of individual self-exploration and self-knowledge are sensed as being immensely threatening by those people who have allied themselves with the drive to control.

Priests and kings, emperors and presidents, and all those who find comfort and safety within the structures maintained by the powerful tend to be disturbed and therefore angered by those who insist on striking off in new directions, ignoring the guidance of appointed leaders. To those in authority, there is the unconscious threat of chaos, the shattering of what is known, familiar, and safe. The response to this threat can take the forms of banishment, burning at the stake, imprisonment, or—at the very least—warnings to keep discoveries private, lest they provoke the self-protective anger of the established order and of those who maintain power through it.

This has been the history of human development on this Earth, a balance maintained—usually with great difficulty and often with violence—between the urge to control and the need to change and grow. And this is the way that we should have been able to have it continue. But the technological growth spurt of the past sixty years has put into our hands a body of knowledge that forever changes the equation.

The great and ancient ways of self-discovering—meditation, lovemaking, music and dancing, singing, ritual, and rhythm—are perhaps now not to be given enough time. The old ways of instructing and helping, by which one generation of insightful and wiser people has always passed on its experience to its children (perhaps with the use of psychoactive plants and chemicals or other teaching tools), may be denied us if the balance shifts too far.

We are now at a time when, if we do not discover a way of acknowledging and accepting the existence of these primal energies within ourselves, we will not be able to learn how to live with them. Until we begin to know, consciously, what there is within our individual and collective psyches, we will be unable to choose wisely. We need to discover that we have centers, cores, I-Am's—whatever name you wish to use—and that this center in each of us has been given the truly incredible gift of choice. We must see that we can weigh, evaluate, understand—and choose. Not just once, but continually. Not unconsciously, but in full awareness. As one example, every time we open our mouths to speak, we choose words on the side of sharing, encouraging, energizing, constructing— or on the side of taking control, asserting power, directing, taking apart. We make use of all aspects of ourselves in everything that we do.

But we must become increasingly aware of what we are and what those energies within us are, and of the choices that are there to be made. And especially, we must be aware of what part of ourselves is actually making each of these choices. For, just as we act on those around us in ways that are loving or destructive, so do we act on ourselves.

We are to ourselves both giver and taker, lover and killer. We fight desperately to continue living one more day, yet we grow within ourselves the seeds of our own punishment. The soul of every one of us mirrors the battle—or the balancing—between the yang and the yin. Consciously or unconsciously, choices will be made. Our own prejudice is strongly toward the conscious, the aware.

The classic arts of India and China present us with paintings, sculptures, and myths that encourage us to face some complex and—to us in the Judeo-Christian West—disturbing truths: that the images of blood and death within us present aspects of both terror and of bliss; that there is a yin and a yang, a light and a dark, a male and a female aspect to everything that lives within us and in everything that surrounds us; and, above all, that being human means being a soul that chooses— consciously or unconsciously—what it will become, what it will do, and what it will ally itself with.

It may well be that choices made by each of us, in full awareness, will be on the side of ending humanity and cleaning up this corner of the universe.

And it may be that we will choose, with love and acceptance, to give the human species a chance to evolve and transform.

It is not possible for us to predict which decision will be made. We argue only for making that decision with as much awareness, as much conscious knowledge, as possible. Let us know just what we are choosing when we make our choices.

Finally, we must begin now to develop our new vocabulary of the human soul, to build a new language with which to communicate this area of experience and knowledge, not only throughout our own society, but across the world.

6 NATURAL SCIENCE AND THE MYSTICAL WORLDVIEW

Albert Hofmann

Albert Hofmann, Ph.D., Dr.Pharm.H.C., Dr.Sc.Nat.H.C., is best known for his serendipitous discovery of LSD and for his chemical work identifying the active principles of the sacred mushroom of Mexico. He was the retired director of research for the Department of Natural Products at Sandoz Pharmaceutical Ltd. in Basel, Switzerland. Dr. Hofmann was a fellow of the World Academy of Science and a member of the Nobel Prize Committee, the International Society of Plant Research, and the American Society of Pharmacognosy. He wrote many scientific papers and several books: *The Botany and Chemistry of Hallucinogens* and *Plants of the Gods* with Richard Evans Schultes, *The Road to Eleusis* with R. G. Wasson and Carl Ruck, *LSD: My Problem Child,* and *Insight/Outlook.*

Born January 11, 1906, Albert celebrated his 100th birthday in excellent health with thousands of grateful admirers at tthe Spirit of Basel—a celebration of his life's work (www.lsd.info/en/home.html). Albert died two years later, on April 29, 2008, four months after his wife, Anita, had passed away. His archives and legacy are managed by Dieter Hagenbach at www.gaiamedia.org.

∾

Nevertheless, this sort of ability of man to separate himself from his environment and to divide and apportion things ultimately led to a wide range of negative and destructive results, because man lost awareness of what he was doing and thus extended the process of division beyond the limits within which it works properly. . . .

It is instructive to consider that the word "health" in English is based on an Anglo-Saxon word "hale" meaning "whole": that is, to be healthy is to be whole, which is, I think, roughly equivalent of the Hebrew "shalem." Likewise, the English "holy" is based on the same root as "whole." All this indicates that man has sensed always that wholeness or integrity is an absolute necessity to make life worth living.

DAVID BOHM, *WHOLENESS AND THE IMPLICATE ORDER*, 1980

WHICH IS TRUE: the picture of reality that natural science presents us, or the one that the mystic experiences in visions? This question can only be asked by one who thinks that natural science and the mystical worldview are mutually exclusive. But that is not the case. On the contrary, natural science and the mystical experience complete each other. To demonstrate that is the purpose of my exposition.

The subject of natural science is the material universe, of which our bodily selves are part. Research in natural science limits itself to the analysis and description of the external world that we can objectively identify with our senses and to inquiry into the laws that govern it.

Such an objective view of nature presupposes a conscious splitting of one's experience of the world into subject and object. Such a dualistic experience of the world first emerged in Europe. This perspective was already apparent in the Judeo-Christian worldview of God high on a throne above creation who commanded humanity to have dominion over nature. The natural sciences are a product of this European mind.

In the beginning of contemporary natural scientific research in the seventeenth century science was still largely related to religion. The scientist confronted nature as creation enlivened by the spirit of God. Kepler recognized the harmony of the world God created in the planetary laws, and in none of the old botanical treatises did the author forget to praise the creator for the wonders of the plant world.

A change of great consequence in the character of natural science took place after the revolutionary discoveries by Galileo and Newton. Research turned more exclusively toward the quantitative, measurable aspects of nature. The qualitative, holistic way of viewing nature, which Goethe defended with his color theory, fell more and more into the background. The quantitative method of natural research demanded increasingly more complicated and refined equipment for its surveys. Physics and chemistry, the disciplines dealing with the measurable aspects of nature, became more prominent. Physical and chemical methods also entered into other areas of natural science, into biology, botany, and zoology.

The grand successes of the natural sciences, especially in the area of physics and chemistry, provided insight into the macrocosmos of the galaxies and into the microcosmos of the atoms. And most importantly, the practical use of the many inventions and discoveries that characterize our era further reinforces today's predominantly materialistic theory of life.

This led to an enormous overrating of the importance of chemistry and physics in the creation. It needs to be recognized that the one-sided belief in the scientific worldview is based on a grave error. All of its content is indeed true, but this content represents only one half of reality, only its material part. All physically and chemically incomprehensible, spiritual dimensions of reality, to which the essential attributes of the living belong, are missing.

The objective here is not to question the validity of scientific perceptions nor to diminish the value of quantitative natural research, but to point out its titanic one-sidedness. Smaller and smaller components of atoms are thought to be the latest reality of our world. The epitome of a purely materialistic worldview is the theory of creation, according to which coincidence and necessity, by means of chemistry and physics, created the cosmos, including all living creatures and plants.

I would like to demonstrate the absurdity of such a theory with a metaphor: the construction of a house. Suppose all the material necessary for the construction of a house existed; the technology and the necessary energy were also at hand. Without the idea of an architect, without the design and its realization according to plan, a house would never be created, even if one would grant chance eons for this enterprise.

If this is true even for a house, which lacks the dimension of life, how much more does it hold true for the living universe, for every flower and insect? The absurdity of such theories about the origin of creation, even if they come from a Nobel Laureate natural scientist like Jacques Monod, is obvious.

In addition to the practical abuse of the knowledge of science, which led to mechanization, industrialization, and destruction of vast areas of life, is the spiritual damage of such nihilistic theories. They deprive life of its spiritual and religious basis and leave man lonely and insecure in a dead, mechanized world.

Nevertheless, the positive effects of natural science on the modern world outweigh the negative ones. I am not primarily thinking of the obviously practical achievements, the progress in medicine, hygiene, longevity, and all the comfort in our daily lives, including television, stereos, computers, and so forth—to which we must add at once that all these comfortable achievements only benefit a small part of the world population. The meaning of natural science in the history of mankind, its revolutionary sense, may lie in the way it has brought about expansion of human consciousness, yielding deeper insight into the essence of reality, the unity of all living beings, and in the belonging of man in the cosmos. As examples of such natural scientific understanding we have gained the following biochemical understandings.

Every higher organism, no matter if plant, animal, or human being, has its origin in one single cell in the fertilized ovum. The smallest units of all living beings, from which all organisms originate, are the cells. The cells of plants, animals, and human beings do not only show similar structures, but they also contain a widely similar chemical composition. Protein, carbohydrate, fat, phosphate, and so forth—these same classes of organic connections physically constitute plant and animal bodies. This uniformity of material composition is connected to the larger metabolistic and energetic cycle of all living beings, in which plants, animals, and humanity are united. The energy that keeps this cycle of life going comes from the sun. The plant, the green carpet of the plant world, is able to—in motherly receptiveness—absorb light as immaterial energy flow and store it in the form of chemically bound energy.

By this process the plant transforms—with the help of chlorophyll as catalyst and light as energy source—water and carbonic acid into organic compositions, into plant substance. This process, called photosynthesis, also delivers through the plant the building blocks of the animal and human organism. All life and all living processes are based energetically on this absorption of light through the plant. The human being's digestive process breaks down plant or animal food, transforming it back into carbonic acid and water. This liberates the same amount of energy as was absorbed in the photosynthesis and makes it available for the body.

Light is the original cosmic energy source. All life, the life of plants, animals, and human beings, is formed and sustained by light. Even the thought process of the human brain is fed by this energy source. Therefore the human mind, our consciousness, represents the highest, most sublime energetic transformation of light. We are light beings; that is not only a mystical experience but scientific knowledge as well. This example should be sufficient to point out that natural science and mysticism contain not contrary but complementary empirical knowledge.

Of all the insights into the nature of objective reality that we owe to natural science, it seems to me that knowledge about the nature of our perception is of especially great significance. It pays to reflect upon the fact that perception by the senses (seeing, hearing, smelling, tasting, feeling) not only mediates our contact with the material outer world but is also the key to the opening of the spiritual world.

Let us recall the words of the mystic poet William Blake (1757–1827):

> *If the doors of perception were cleansed,*
> *everything would appear to man as it is, infinite.*

To demonstrate the relationship of the external material world to the internal psycho-spiritual world it may be useful to compare it to the way picture and sound are created in a television broadcast.

The material world in the outer sphere works as a sender, sending out optic and acoustic waves and delivering touch, taste, and smell signals. The reception is formed by the consciousness inside each individual, where the impulses received by the sense organs, the antennas, are transformed into sensual and mental experiences of the outer world.

If one of the two is missing, the sender or the receiver, no human reality would occur; the television screen would stay blank and without sound.

What follows is based on scientific knowledge about human physiology concerning the function as receiver as well as about the mechanism of reception and experience of reality.

The antennas of human receivers are our five sense organs. The antenna for optical images, the eye, is able to receive electromagnetic waves, light waves, which produce an image on the retina that corresponds to the object from which those waves came. From there the nervous impulses that correspond to the image are transmitted through the optic nerve into the optical center of the brain, where the electrophysiological energetic occurrence, the subjective psychic phenomenon, the vision, results. Vision is a psychic phenomenon that is not further explainable scientifically.

It is important to realize that our eye and the inner psychic screen only use a very small sector from the enormous spectrum of electromagnetic waves to make the outer world visible. Out of the electromagnetic spectrum of waves, which covers wavelengths from billionths of millimeters, the range of X-rays, to radio waves meters in length, our optical apparatus only responds to the very small range of 0.4 to 0.7 thousandths of millimeters. Only this very little sector can be received by our eyes and be perceived as light.

Within the visible wave range, we are able to perceive the different wavelengths as various colors. It is important to realize that no color exists in the outer world. In general, one is not aware of this fundamental fact. What is objectively present in the outer world of an object that we see as colored is exclusively *substance,* which sends out electromagnetic vibrations of certain wavelengths. If an object reflects light that falls on it in waves of 0.4 thousandths of millimeters, then we say that it is "blue." If it sends out waves of 0.7 thousandths of millimeters, we name that optical result as "red." But it is impossible to determine whether or not all people have the same color experience within the reception of a particular wavelength. The perception of color is purely a psychic, subjective experience, which takes place in the inner world of an individual. The colorful world, as we see it, does not objectively exist outside, but originates on the psychic screen in the inside of the individual person.

In the acoustic world, analogous relationships exist between a sender in the outer world and a receiver in the inner world. The antenna for acoustic signals, the ear, in its function as part of the human receiver, likewise shows only a restricted range of reception. Like colors, sounds do not objectively exist. What objectively exists in the process of hearing are, again, waves, wavelike condensations and expansions of the air, which are registered by the membrane of the ear and are transformed into the psychic experience of sound in the hearing center of the brain.

Our receiver for acoustic waves perceives the range of twenty vibrations per second up to twenty thousand vibrations, which correspond to form the deepest up to the highest audible sounds.

The other aspects of reality that are made accessible by the remaining three senses of taste, smell, and touch originate as well from an interaction between material and energy senders in the outer world and a psychic receiver in the inner world of the individual person. The sensations of taste, smell, and touch are, like colors and sounds, not objectively identifiable. They only exist on the psychic monitor inside of the person.

From this knowledge it follows that the world as we perceive it with our eyes and the other sense organs presents a reality specific to the human being—a reality that is determined by the abilities and restrictions of the human sensory organs. Animals, with their different sensory organs, with antennas that react to different impulses, and with different receivers, have a different consciousness, which lacks psychomental-spiritual perception and the ability to love. They see and experience the outer world completely differently, which means that they live in a different reality.

We can only see, hear, smell, taste, and feel as much of the outer world as we can perceive with our restricted senses. Only that much is real for us, only that much becomes reality. Matthias Claudius expressed that poetically in his beautiful poem, where it says, "So there are indeed some things that we easily laugh at, because our eyes do not see them."

The sender and receiver metaphor brings to light that the seemingly objective image of the outer world, which we refer to as "reality," is, as a matter of fact, a subjective image. It is a fundamental fact that the screen is located on the inside of every human being. All human beings carry their own personally created image of reality. It is their true image of the world, because it is what they can perceive with their own eyes and with the other senses.

The screen is not external, but dwells within each person. All people carry their own personal image of reality within—created by their private receiver. This image reveals the world-creating potency that is every individual's due. All human beings are the creators of their own world, because simply and solely within do the earth, the colorful life on her, the stars, and the sky become reality.

That sounds very mystical, *is* mystical, but in the same way it is natural scientific truth, a fact understandable and verifiable by everybody. Founded on this truly cosmogonic ability is the true dignity of the individual; in it lies the actual freedom and responsibility of every human being, which reaches far beyond the significance of his political freedom and responsibility.

When I realize what reality is objectively outside and what happens subjectively within me, then I know better what I can change in my life, where I have a choice, and consequently for what I am responsible and, on the other hand, what lies beyond my power and my will or has to be accepted as unchangeable fact. It is I who give color to the objects that in the outer world are only formed material, but through my attention and love, I also give them meaning. That is not only valid for the lifeless environment but also for the living creatures, for plants and animals, and also for my fellow men.

This clarification of responsibility is an invaluable aid to life.

I would like to point to one further insight that the sender-receiver model conveys. The model demonstrates the fundamental fact that reality is not a clearly defined condition, but the result of continuous processes, consisting of a continuous input of material and energetic signals from the outer world and its continuous decoding and transformation into psychic experiences and perceptions in the inner world. Reality is a dynamic process; it is constantly created new in every moment. Actual reality is consequently only in the here and now, in the moment.

That explains why the child, who lives much more in the moment than the adult, perceives a real image of the world. There is more reality in the childhood paradise than in the world experience of adults. Within that lies a deep meaning. Why else would Jesus have said the kingdom of heaven is theirs?

The experience of true reality in the moment is a main goal of mysticism. Childlike and mystical worldviews meet here. Here is a poem from the baroque era by Andreas Gryphius:

> Mine are not the years, that time took from me.
> Mine are not the years, that perchance might come.
> The moment is mine, and if I take care of it,
> It will be mine, that which made time and eternity.

If reality was not the result of uninterrupted changes, but was a stationary condition, then there would not only be no moment, there would also be no time, because sensation of time is created only through the perception of change. The processlike character of material reality creates time.

In conclusion, I would like to explain a further insight that arises from the sender-receiver model of reality. It is an insight regarding communication. I don't mean communication disseminated by mass media, but the existential basis of communication, given that we are physical beings.

The sender-receiver model shows how we, as receiver of material and energetic impulses of the outer world, experience the outer world. We are not only recipients of messages from the outer world but also, as part of this outer world, senders. As I am recipient for the messages of my fellow man, so am I, on the other hand, sender for him. I can convey my concerns to him, even a purely spiritual one, a thought or my love, only through that which characterizes the sender, namely, through material and energy, through my body.

A wordless understanding as well, which manifests itself in a look or tender touch, can simply only be expressed through material eyes, material fingers, through the material bodies of the loving partners. Without substance and energy, communication would not be possible. That is not only true for the relationship between humans, but also for cosmic relationships. The creator as well can transmit his messages only through his vast sender, through creation, through the material cosmos.

Paracelsus, the great doctor, natural researcher, and philosopher of the Renaissance, called creation a book written by the finger of God that we need to learn to read. It contains the message firsthand. It is the message of the infinity of the starry sky and the beauty of our Earth with all its exquisite creatures. Natural science always decodes further new texts from this message, and the religious man experiences in meditation, in the mystical view, its totality and within that the wonder of our existence. This could become the basis of a new, Earth-sweeping spirituality. In that spirit I would like to conclude with this quotation from the script "Sadhana" by Rabindranath Tagore, translated by Frauke Zajac and Nina Graboi:

Through the progress of natural science the totality of the world and our oneness with it becomes clearer to our spirit. When this realization of the complete unity is not only an intellectual realization, when it opens up our whole being to the light of total consciousness, then it becomes a radiant joy, an all encompassing love.

PSYCHEDELIC SOCIETY

Terence McKenna

Terence McKenna was an author and explorer who spent twenty-five years studying the ontological foundations of shamanism and the ethno-pharmacology of spiritual transformation. He traveled extensively in the Asian and New World tropics, becoming specialized in the shamanism and ethno-medicine of the Amazon Basin. With his brother Dennis McKenna, he wrote *The Invisible Landscape* and *Psilocybin: The Magic Mushroom Growers' Guide.* Terence also wrote *Food of the Gods,* a study of the impact of psychotropic plants on human culture and evolution; *The Archaic Revival,* a book of essays and conversations; and *True Hallucinations,* a narrative of spiritual adventure in the jungles of the Colombian Amazon. Before dying of brain cancer on April 3, 2000, in addition to his books, he left an incomparable legacy articulating the ineffable, which is available throughout the Internet, especially on YouTube. (An excellent film about him can be found at http://terence-mckenna-movie.tumblr.com.) This talk was transcribed by Peter Stafford in January 1985. For Terence's final word, please see www.levity.com/eschaton/index.html.

*In rare instances, an LSD subject can have the feeling that
his consciousness has expanded to encompass the totality*

of life on this planet, including all humankind and the entirety of flora and fauna, from unicellular organisms to highly differentiated species. An individual can identify with the phylogenetic evolution of life in all its complexity and reach an intuitive understanding of the underlying biological laws. He can explore the factors that influence the origin of a new species or are responsible for their extinction. . . . Similar insights can be experienced in regard to the interaction of different life forms in all the permutations of their synergisms and antagonisms within the framework of planetary ecology. . . . Experiences of this kind can result in an enhanced awareness of and sensitivity to ecological problems related to technological development and rapid industrialization.

STANISLAV GROF, *REALMS OF*
THE HUMAN UNCONSCIOUS, 1975

I WANT TO talk tonight about the notion of a psychedelic society. When I spoke in Santa Barbara at a psychedelics conference in May 1983 my contact lenses failed me at a critical point in my lecture and I simply had to wing it. Later when I played this tape back I heard the phrase "psychedelic society." I never used it before consciously in a lecture. But because I had said it and because there had been a ripple of resonance to it from the people there, I began to think about it and this evening I will generally assess what it might mean for us.

When I think of psychedelic society that notion implies creating a society that lives in light of the Mystery of Being. In other words, problems and solutions should be displaced from the central role they have had in social organizations, and Mysteries—*irreducible Mysteries*—should be in their place. In the 1920s the British entomologist J. B. S. Haldane said in an essay, "The universe may not only be stranger than we suppose; it may be stranger than we *can* suppose."

I suggest that as we look back over human history every pinnacle of civilization—whether it be Mayan, or Greco-Roman, or the Sung dynasty—has believed that it was in possession of an accurate description of the cosmos and of man's relationship to it. This seems to go along with the full flowering of a civilization. But from the point of view of our present civilization we regard all those earlier conceptions as at worst quaint, at best half right. We congratulate ourselves that our civilization at last has its finger on the real description of what is going on.

I think this is an error and that actually what blinds us, or makes historical progress very difficult, is our lack of awareness that our beliefs have grown obsolete and should be put aside. A psychedelic society would abandon belief systems for direct experience. This is I think much of the problem of the modern dilemma: direct experience has been discounted, and in its place all kinds of belief systems have been erected.

I would prefer a kind of intellectual anarchy where whatever was pragmatically applicable was brought to bear on any situation—where belief was understood as a self-limiting function. Because, you see, if you believe something, you are automatically precluded from believing its opposite, which means that a degree of your human freedom has been forfeited in the act of committing yourself to this belief.

I maintain that it is pointless to have beliefs, because if the universe really is stranger than we suppose, what we need is a return to what in the sixteenth century was called the Baconian method—which means not the elaboration of fantastic thought constructs that explain nature, but merely a phenomenological cataloging of what we experience. Computer networks and psychedelic drugs and the increased availability of information in the world have actually made possible the evolution of new information states that never existed before. We are processing these new opportunities at a very slow rate because we are hindered by ideology.

Freudian and Jungian models of the psychedelic experience see it as a stripping away of resistance revealing hidden and complex emotions, motives, and belief systems. This notion has been replaced by the shamanic model of hallucinogenic experience. This model holds that archaic peoples have deputized special members of society to probe hidden information domains using psychedelic drugs. The information extracted from these domains is then used to guide and direct the society.

I am interested in this second model. I've spent time in the Amazon and am familiar with the operational mechanics of shamanism and shamanic personalities. I believe that the psychedelic experience looms larger even than the institution of shamanism. We are facing a unique opportunity, which is the flip side of the global culture crisis.

Our ability to destroy ourselves is the mirror image of our ability to save ourselves. What is lacking is a clear vision of what should be done. What should be done is certainly not the accumulation of ever-larger thermonuclear arsenals and the promotion of all kinds of primate game-playing—the sort that Tim Leary was well versed in denouncing. What needs to be done is that our fundamental ontological conceptions of reality have to be remade. We need a new language, and in order to have a new language we must have a new reality. It's a kind of uroboric equation or a bootstrap situation. A new reality will generate a new language. A new language will make a new reality legitimate and a part of this reality.

The psychedelic substances can be conceived of as points on an informational grid. They provide new perspectives on reality, and when you reconnect all the points of view that you have collected regarding reality, then a reasonably applicable model of reality begins to appear.

I think this reasonably applicable model of reality—what Wittgenstein called something that is "true enough"—is what we are looking for. The "true enough" mapping of experience onto theory is what we are looking for, but experience must be made primary. The language of the self must be made primary.

What I am advocating is that we each take responsibility for the cultural transformation by realizing that it is not something that will be disseminated from the top down. It is something that each of us can contribute to by attempting to live as far into the future as possible. We must get rid of the conceptions of the twentieth century. We must transcend the historical moment and become exemplars of humanity at the end of time.

Those of you who attended my lecture this afternoon concerning time know that I believe that liberation—or let's even say "decency"—as a human quality is a resonance and anticipation of this future perfected state of humanity. We can will the perfect future into being by becoming microcosms of the perfect future, no longer casting blame outward onto institutions or hierarchies of responsibility or control, but realizing the opportunity is here, the responsibility is here, and the two may never be congruent again. The salvation of your immortal soul may depend on what you do with the opportunity life places before you.

So, what do we do with the opportunity? What does it mean to say, in operational terms, "Live as far into the future as you can"? It means taking a position vis-à-vis the emergent hyper-dimensional reality. It does not necessarily mean becoming a psychedelic drug user yourself, but it does mean admitting to the possibility. If you feel the heroic potential within to be one of the experiencers—one of the pioneers—then you know what to do. If on the other hand you feel lost in the abyss—you feel what William Blake called "the falling into eternal death," falling from the spiral of being that connects one incarnation to another—then you orient yourself toward the psychedelic experience as a source of information.

A mirror image of the psychedelic experience has emerged in the integrated hardware and software comprising the computer networks. The Internet and the World Wide Web are, paradoxically enough, a deeply feminizing influence on society. It is in hardware/software development that the unconscious is actually becoming conscious. It is as though we took the Platonic bon mot—"If God did not exist, man would invent him"—and said, "If the unconscious did not exist, humanity will invent it in the form of these vast networks that are able to transfer and transform information."

This is, in fact, what we are caught up in: the transforming of information. We have not physically changed in the last forty thousand years. The human type was established well before the end of the last glaciation. Change that previously operated in the biological realm is now operating in the realm of culture. And we are shedding cultural assumptions concerning our vision of the unitary mystery at a faster and faster rate as we try to accommodate ourselves to the unfolding of that mystery which lies ahead of us in time. It is that process that is casting a vast shadow of fatedness back over the entire experience of human history.

Previous to our own era, the only word that could be applied to this force that is bringing people together, causing birth and death, tearing down and erecting civilizations, was God, and it was imagined as a self-conscious force that was leaning into the world like a cat into a fishbowl and making things happen. Now we have a different notion—a notion of a vector system where forces over a large area are oriented toward a very small space, and this dense micro-sector of space/time is what history is. It is an inrushing toward what the Buddhists call "the realm of the densely-packed," a transformational realm where the opposites are unified.

History is that realm where the body is finally interiorized and the mind is finally exteriorized. The way I think of the mind is as a fourth-dimensional organ of your body. You can't see it because it is in the fourth dimension, but you experience a lower-dimensional sectioning of it in the phenomenon of consciousness. But that is only a partial sectioning of it, the way an ellipse is a partial picture of a cone.

The growth of information systems is only a mirroring in masculine hardware of what already exists in nature as a fact. It is up to us to hone our intuitions and to become aware of this preexisting system of communication and wiring so that we can step away from the dualisms that separate us from each other and from the world. We need to realize that there is a gene swarm—not a set of species—on the earth; that half the time you think you are thinking you are actually listening; that ideas are remarkably slippery creatures that are very difficult to trace to their origin; and that we really are one-on-one and all together in a dimension that is not as accessible as you might wish to be congealed (as Joyce comments in *Finnegan's Wake*).

The psychedelics are a red-hot, social/ethical issue precisely because they are deconditioning agents. They will raise doubts in you if you are a Hassidic rabbi, a Marxist anthropologist, or an altar boy because their business is to dissolve belief systems. They do this very well, and then they leave you with the raw datum of experience, what William James called—talking of infantile experience—"a blooming, buzzing confusion."

Out of that you reconstruct the world, and you need to understand that this reconstruction is a dialogue where your decisions—the projection of your grammar onto the intellectual space in front of you—is going to gel into a mode of being. We all create our own universe because we are all operating with our own private languages, which are only very crudely translatable into any other person's language. There is even a physical analog to this, which will further reinforce this notion of our separateness and our uniqueness.

Your picture of the world impinging on your eyes is made of photons. Photons are tiny wave packets so closely circumscribed interjectionally that they can be thought of as particles. That means that every single photon that falls on the back of my eye is different from every single photon that falls on the back of any one of your eyes. This means that I am relying 100 percent on a different section of the world than any one of you are to get a picture of it. And yet we are sitting here with the naive assumption that our pictures of the world differ only by our perspective within the space of the room.

We have numerous extremely naive assumptions like this built into our thinking. Our most venerable explanatory engines—such as "science"—happen also to be our oldest explanatory engines. Therefore they have built into them the most naive and unexamined assumptions. "Science," for instance, we can demolish in thirty seconds. "Science" tells you that a set of conditions will create a given effect and that every time that set of conditions is in place that effect will be found to obtain. The only place this happens is in laboratories. Our experience isn't like that. A contact with a person is always different. The experience of making love, having a meal, riding a bus—these things are always different. It is their uniqueness in fact—the uniqueness that pervades all being—that makes it bearable at all. Yet "science" is willing to tell you that the only things worth describing are those phenomena that can be repeatedly triggered. This is because these are the only phenomena that science can describe, and that's the name of the game as far as it is concerned.

But we need to claim our freedom—to take advantage of the tiny moment between immense abysses of unknowability—perhaps death, perhaps other reincarnations, perhaps transitions into other life forms. These things we don't know or understand, but in the moment of being human, we have a unique opportunity to figure them out. And I have faith that it is possible—sometime, somewhere—to have a conversation. Perhaps no progress would be made until the ninth hour in which reality could be literally pulled to pieces, beyond the point of reconstruction.

There is definitely an anti-humanist tendency in all systems. Ludwig von Bertalanfe, who was the inventor of general systems theory, said, "People are not machines, but in every situation where they are given the choice they will behave like machines." We all fall into patterns. We then hold those patterns ever more tightly. They cannot be violated, and this happens on the thought level.

We are now at the cresting of the historical wave of this kind of uptightness, uptightness that stretches back millennia. I hope we have come to the end of this phase. Whether you buy into my own peculiar, apocalyptarian transformative vision involving 2012, or whether you just can tell by looking around you that the shit may soon hit the fan, I think that we can agree that we have come to some kind of an impasse. What is going to come out of this situation is either going to be a great deal of dislocation in the biosphere, the invalidation of intelligence as an adaptation of biology, and our extinction, or we are going to become—as James Joyce dreamed we could—"man made dirigible," in other words, the exteriorization of the soul, the interiorization of the body.

In this process, everything is going to be challenged. The very notion of humanness is going to be challenged. We are on the brink, through genetic manipulation of DNA, of taking control of the human form, of being able to extend the notion of art inward into the human body and form. Are we classicists? Shall we each be an Adonis and a Persephone? Or what are we? Are we surrealists? Shall I be a potato and you a burning giraffe? These are decisions that will have to be faced. I smile as I speak but these are the important questions.

And the vertical gain notion we see in the metaphors applied to psychedelic experience: consciousness expansion, getting high, psychedelic tripping, shamanic flight. It's like the hallucinogens are the feminine, software, formative, leading edge of what is happening. Coming along behind that is the hardware, the masculine engineering mentality.

This will continue until the leading edge outdistances the engineering mentality through breakthrough. This is what the shamanic hope is: that we can find a way to use chemicals in our bodies, use our voices, our thoughts, and our hands upon ourselves and each other; to transform ourselves without technology; to move into the realm of the imagination—on the natch, as it were—with an interiorized psychopharmacologically applied technology that frees us in the imagination.

At the same time that this is going on, the engineering mentality is going to set human societies in orbit around the earth, moon, and the near planets. But there is a catch here for the engineering mentality, which is that the very void that surrounds the planets exemplifies the enfolding, abyssal, feminine element. It is the mysterious Mama matrix of *Finnegan's Wake*. The mysterious Mama matrix is the universe, and there is no escaping that fact. But I think the engineering mentality,

which will seek to change man into his machines, will have to be coun-
terpoised by the psychedelic, earth-oriented, imagination-oriented side
of consciousness, which will create then the potential for the spiritual marriage that will be the alchemical incubation of a new form of
humanity, and this is not far away.

It can't be far away. It is a personal responsibility incumbent upon
all of us to act to help create it. There is a definite obligation to examine the possibility of action and to think clearly about self and other,
language and world, past and future. For too long we have lived in a
world defined by geography. If you are born in India, you will find out
that the cosmos is one way. If you are born in Brooklyn, you find out
it is something else. We need to transcend these localized grids of biological fate, which make us what we are but don't want to be. We can
claim this higher level of freedom by the simple act of paying attention
to being.

We must begin to send out ideological visions rather than be the
consumers of them. We need to turn off the virtual internal televi-
sions, which are hooking us in to the tired cultural assumptions dic-
tated from the Pentagon, Madison Avenue, and the corporate state. We
need instead to turn on our modems and to begin to interact with like-
minded people throughout the world and establish this new intellectual
order, which will be the salvation of the biosphere, I firmly believe. The
Internet concretizes our collectivity, finally allowing people to feel the
interrelatedness of their fates—to feel this interrelatedness as a thing
that transcends national divisions, ideological divisions. The Internet
allows each of us to recover the experience of being part of the human
family.

No reconstruction of society can be done without psychedelics because we have drifted so long without them. Surely we are the
products of societies that have gone longer without psychedelics than
any other culture in the world. It's been two thousand years since the
Mystery was real at Eleusis, and in that two thousand years we have
wandered far, far into dysfunction and confusion. But we are the prodi-

gal sons. We can redeem the ideal of shamanism from pretechnological social stasis and actually project it, perfect it, and travel with it out to the stars.

And if we don't, everything is lost. There is no standing still. There is only risk and commitment to these millennial aspirations and cultural goals, goals that have the potential to restore meaning and direction to our civilization. If this is not done we will fritter away our opportunity and be left prey to the destruction and the horrors of the typical future scenario.

8 A CONVERSATION WITH R. GORDON WASSON

Robert Forte

R. Gordon Wasson began the field of ethnomycology when he and his wife, Valentina, "discovered" the role of entheogenic mushrooms in the religious practices of societies throughout the world. Though a banker by profession, Mr. Wasson became a research fellow of the Botanical Museum of Harvard University, and the New York Botanical Garden named him honorary research associate and honorary life manager. Comprising his prodigious literary output are the classic books *Mushrooms, Russia and History* (1957); *Soma: Divine Mushroom of Immortality* (1969); *Maria Sabina and Her Mazatec Mushroom Velada* (1974); *The Road to Eleusis* (1978); *The Wondrous Mushroom* (1980); and *Persephone's Quest: Entheogens and the Origin of Religion* (1986). Gordon Wasson died on December 23, 1986.

> *He was most certainly a "gentleman of the old school."*
> *Whether in his New York or London clubs or in the hills of*
> *Oaxaca, he knew how to respect those with who he came in*

contact. But his strict meticulousness in every aspect of his activities knew no bounds and even occasionally irritated a few scholars who did not understand this basic characteristic of his being. He could not bear sloppiness, especially in writing, and showed no patience with mediocrity. I have never known a man more meticulous in his bearing, his speech, his writing and his thinking. . . . Above all, he was intrinsically gentle and humble, a part of his nature that became ever more obvious the longer one knew and worked with him. Always self-effacing, he shunned publicity—a characteristic which, unfortunately, some who did not know him personally interpreted as snobbish aloofness, a trait completely foreign to his personality.

RICHARD EVANS SCHULTES,
THE SACRED MUSHROOM SEEKER:
ESSAYS FOR R. GORDON WASSON, 1990

*[**Note to the Reader:** Unlike the previous chapters, there is a notes section at the end of this essay that contains information beyond mere reference citations. These notes provide important background and context for R. Gordon Wasson's life and times. —Ed.]*

THIS CONVERSATION TOOK place at Mr. Wasson's home in Danbury, Connecticut, in October 1985, fourteen months before Gordon passed away. Gordon Wasson was a Wall Street banker, a vice president of the J. P. Morgan Trust. Mycology was his pastime until he retired from banking in 1963, then, as he puts it, he "got down to real business." Over the next twenty years Wasson authored six books in the field of ethnomycology and dozens of scholarly articles unveiling the origin and phenomenology of some of humanity's greatest religious mysteries. He became a research fellow of the Botanical Museum of Harvard University, and Yale awarded him their esteemed Veblen Prize. But the full significance of his research has yet to be appreciated by modern society. It would be illegal today in America to do what Gordon and his wife accomplished when they found the sacred mushroom and brought it back to the Western world. In 1957 they wrote:

> How amusing it has been to discover in mycophobia the willing, nay determined subservience of many Europeans to a simple tabu such as we like to associate with primitive peoples, a subservience to emotional responses that seem to stem back to the days when our ancestors found themselves face to face with the miraculous powers of the sacred mushroom! The secret lost, the tabu survives. Like the tribes our anthropologists study, we cling to our tabus and seek to justify them by rationalizing them. Few men want freedom, however they may talk. But then again perhaps man is free in his choice when he chooses to abide within the confines of his unreason. (Wasson and Wasson 1957)

Robert Forte: *First let me say what a pleasure it is to be here and to see you again, Mr. Wasson. You are looking well, and though you say your health has not been well, your appearance doesn't show it. It is a special honor to interview you. I want to ask you first about the beginning of your career in mycology. Your first discovery was that you, typical of your Anglo-Saxon heritage, were raised in ignorance of the world of mushrooms, with an aversion, a loathing, even a fear of them, while your wife, Valentina Pavlovna, typical of her Russian heritage, grew up with a knowledge of the common mushrooms and a certain fondness for them. These differing attitudes propelled you both on your study. You later coined the words "mycophobia" and "mycophilia" to describe these contrasting attitudes. Could you say something about this difference?*

R. Gordon Wasson: After studying the matter for almost a generation we found first of all that the difference was not a personal thing. It was not *I* and it was not *my wife*. It was all Russians and all Anglo-Saxons that felt in these divergent ways. It prompted us to say we should look into that to see why this was so. We studied it for about twenty years, and then around about 1939 we sat down together to decide whether we should go on with it. We were both very busy with earning a living—making a go of it. My wife was then a pediatrician. Her practice was constantly interrupted by the travels with me. I was sent down to Argentina by the bank for a year, and we went together, naturally, as I was trying to make a go of it by banking. It was then not so sure a thing as it became later. So we were working hard, and we did not wish to waste any more time on mushrooms. But if there were anything really important in it, we wished to go on with it. At this meeting toward the end of the thirties we both discovered that the other one had a secret, a secret that we were too shy to express to each other. And the secret was that religion lay behind it, behind those who hated mushrooms, those who feared them, and those who loved them, as the Russians loved them.

RF: *To what extent do you think this difference is due to the hallucinogenic potency of some mushrooms?*

RGW: To the entheogenic potency you mean?

RF: *Would you clarify the distinction?*

RGW: Yes. "Hallucination" means "a lie." A hallucination is nothing. I don't like the word. I do not think it should be used. "Entheogen" is a much better word. A committee of us headed by Professor Carl Ruck, a classical scholar at Boston University, devised that word and we all adopted it unanimously rather than "hallucinogen" for those plant substances revered by early man for their potency, for their ability to command respect. *Amanita muscaria* is the main fungal entheogen, but the *Psilocybe* genus often has entheogenic properties. "Entheogen" means simply "God generated within you"!

RF: *So "hallucination" implies something false, or not real.*

RGW: Yes. It is all right for Tim Leary and their ilk, they can use it, but it is a shabby word, "hallucination." It is not a hallucination what you experience when you consume the mushrooms that produce visions and that speak.

RF: *To what extent do you think that mycophobia and mycophilia are due to the entheogenic properties of some mushrooms?*

RGW: Well, I think it is due to that. Do you disagree with me?

RF: *No. I think it could be another instance of the great ambivalence we see toward the sacred throughout history. There is great attraction for the sacred, and so much about it becomes taboo. How long were you involved in mycology before you came upon the sacred mushrooms of Mexico?*

RGW: In 1952 we received a clipping from Robert Graves,[1] a clipping that he found in the house journal of Ciba (*Chemische Industrie Basel*) in New York. It reported the discovery of a mushroom cult in Mexico. The friars who accompanied the conquerors into Mexico reported on this cult. Though they did not say much about it, they were very brief, what they said was accurate and good, as good as you could expect it to be in that generation because there was no mycology at that time. They did not know one mushroom from another.

Deborah Harlow:* *Mr. Wasson, you say that it was in 1952 that you received this communication from Mr. Graves, but it was in 1939 that you and Mrs. Wasson had this hunch about religion and the mushrooms. Whence came this hunch?*

RGW: Well, it came from our studying mushrooms since 1927. We had got some hints of the Asiatic practice of eating the *Amanita muscaria*. Unfortunately in English we have no word to express this mushroom. This is a nameless mushroom in English. We are deprived of the privilege of talking about it familiarly. We have to use the botanical name *Amanita muscaria*. This is a reflection I think of our antipathy to all

---

*Deborah Harlow, at the time of the interview, was a graduate student at Harvard University.

mushrooms, and particularly to the *Amanita muscaria,* which is a very great mushroom and which has not been exhaustively studied at all!

RF: *Were you or your wife particularly religious before you began your quest?*

RGW: No, we were not particularly religious. I am not particularly religious yet. But religious, well, mildly religious. My father was an Episcopal clergyman.[2]

RF: *So this was a hobby you were involved in?*

RGW: We didn't regard it as a hobby. We would not have devoted so much time to it if it were a hobby. But we pursued it with our left hand so to speak. She was busy trying to get going in medicine, and I was first in newspaper work and later in banking.

RF: *You relinquished your fear of mushrooms quite early on then?*

RGW: Oh yes, my wife won that battle.

RF: *You had read about the existence of the divine mushroom?*

RGW: In time we had learned about the travelers in eastern Siberia in the eighteenth and nineteenth century; they had found this practice. They were astonished, and they were disgusted by the "filth" of these paleo-Siberian tribesmen, and contemptuous of their culture, and naturally of this practice of eating the mushrooms and getting into a state of "intoxication" they thought. But some of the observers were very talented, and their testimony is well worth reading carefully. The natives said after they tried alcohol that they preferred the mushroom. It did not have the aftereffects that drunkenness leads you to, and they liked it better. No one paid any attention to them. Very smugly the Europeans thought they were doing them a favor by introducing them to alcohol.

RF: *So your first inkling of a divine mushroom was the* Amanita muscaria *in Siberia?*

RGW: Yes, that is the first we heard of it. Then the next time I found the *Amanita* was when I began my travels after my wife's death in 1958. Well, of course, we traveled together to Mexico every year in the fifties, and all our discoveries there were made in that time. But they were different kinds of mushrooms.

Then, after Mexico, I wished to get some taste of what was to be the case in Asia. So when I retired in 1963—as soon as I retired—the very same night, I flew to San Francisco and boarded a freighter that took me to Auckland in New Zealand. Then I went to Australia, New Guinea, and finally to India. In India I got a hold of the *Rig Veda* and began to read it. The ninth mandala is entirely devoted to the sacred plant *soma,* and that was when we got down to real business.

First of all, I asked Professor Ingalls[3] at Harvard to recommend someone, a graduate student, who could help me with questions about Sanskrit. He said that he had a girl, Wendy Doniger O'Flaherty, who would be marvelous at giving me advice. But there was no point in asking her because she would refuse. She was "too full of life," he said. But I said, "Why don't you let her decide?" And she accepted at once with enthusiasm, though she had never met me. Anyway, we hit it off very well. Our correspondence was supreme. She was in Cambridge, Massachusetts, and I in my home in New York, and later, after she had taken her Ph.D. degree at Harvard, she went to Oxford where she took another degree in Sanskrit studies, and is now a professor at the University of Chicago.

RF: *Before we get too far into the soma question I should ask you more about your experiences in Mexico. What was your attitude when you were going into this? Often Westerners have had a condescending attitude toward the religious practices of so-called primitive cultures. What were you thinking when you learned of this Mexican mushroom and were going there to find out?*

RGW: Well, I think that the attitude of many Americans, especially anthropologists—now I do not wish to say anything too severe but I found anthropologists, many of the younger men—think that religion is a nonsubject. They are not interested in it, and they do not inquire about it. They have any number of other things that interest them more. Kinship relationships. They will devote any amount of time to know who you can marry and who you cannot marry and such futile subjects as that. But when it comes to religion, it does not exist for them. And they also have a contempt for the missionaries that may be down in that neighborhood. They feel that they are pursuing an entirely wrong attitude. Of course the missionaries are trying to convert the natives, and sometimes they do it rather unwisely I feel. But when they are sincere, they learn what the attitude of the native is toward religion. That interested them mightily, whereas with some of the anthropologists, it was a nonsubject. Well, I feel entirely sympathetic with the missionaries. They, the intelligent missionaries, learned the attitude toward religion of the natives, and they did not despise the local religions.

We spent endless effort to publish our book, *Maria Sabina and Her Mazatec Mushroom Velada*, endless effort with the Cowans, George and Florence Cowan—they were missionaries there. For fifteen years we worked on that text to publish it. We had to take it down from my tape into living Mazatec and spell it out in the manner that the Cowans and their associates devised for writing this unwritten language, and publishing it, line for line, in Spanish, English, and Mazatec, giving the left-hand page to Mazatec, and line for line, the other languages. Endless effort we spent! And I have not noticed that it has had any reaction at all from anybody! But I am as proud of that as I am of anything I have written. It is available in two editions. One is the expensive one with records, the other has cassette tapes accompanying it.

RF: *So your attitude going into Mexico was an appreciative attitude?*

RGW: Well, I went in there to see what this cult was, and I wished to learn about it, and I did not wish to ignore it.

RF: *You reported that Maria Sabina lamented divulging the secret of the mushrooms to you because many more foreigners followed. . . .*[4]

RGW: Not only foreigners, but Mexicans also came to explore it. Mexicans could have learned about it on their own, in the friars' accounts of the sixteenth century, which are fascinating. Those old friars! Well, some of them were bigots, but many of them were worthwhile people.

RF: *You first learned about this cult though Robert Graves?*

RGW: Yes, he sent me that clipping from the trade journal of Ciba and then from Richard Evans Schultes[5] who had then published two articles (Schultes 1939, 1940), which I learned of in 1952. He had published them in 1939 and '40—many years before—but then everything was swallowed up in the war. He went to the Amazon.

RF: *When did you and Mrs. Wasson go to Mexico?*

RGW: In 1953 we took part in a velada, as it has come to be called in English. A "midnight vigil" is what it means, or a "vigil at night." The mushrooms are taken only at night. You do not talk about them in the public square or in mixed company. You talk about it only when you are at home and you are one-to-one with your hostess or some other person. That is the way you talk about them. That was Maria Sabina's dismay. There were so many people that they became common. People misbehaved in her velada. They would drink alcohol. Think of it! Drinking alcohol and taking the mushroom together! Shocking! Not that I am opposed to alcohol [see note 2].

RF: *What was really a magnificent contribution to anthropology and to the history of religions, a crowning achievement for Mrs. Wasson and yourself, became then a source of great sadness for you.*

RGW: Yes. Well, we had foreseen this. We said that we wished to give it as dignified a presentation and as worthy a presentation as it deserved, and we did do so. I wrote an article in *Life* (Wasson 1957), which was restrained.

RF: *Though Maria Sabina may have thought that the mushroom velada* *was ruined due to the intrusion of the white people, another way to see it is that the mushroom was rescued from obscurity. Many more now have the opportunity to learn about this.*

RGW: Yes, of course inevitably it would have disappeared. The whole rite would have disappeared, and it might have disappeared unnoticed. This was a way in which it could be preserved by us, for posterity.

RF: *Around this time you began your association with Dr. Albert Hofmann,[6] whom you contacted to identify the psychoactive constituents of these mushrooms.*

RGW: Yes, that is right. That is, Roger Heim, the director of the Museum National d'Histoire Naturelle, did. He had previous experience with Albert Hofmann. When Heim was unsuccessful in analyzing the mushrooms in Paris, he sent them to Albert Hofmann. Albert Hofmann had been longing to get them. He had wondered how he could reach me to get the mushrooms to do the chemical work. It turned out to be a much simpler job than he expected because the chemicals in the mushroom are related to the chemicals in ergot.

RF: *I understand that the CIA was right on your trail going down to Mexico. Could you say more about their interest in this?*

RGW: Well, I won't say anything very strong or interesting. The CIA thought that they might be able to apply this to war, and they wished to investigate it. They called me up and asked whether I would work with them, and I said, "Give me a day to think it over." I called them up the next day and said I would not. It would tie my hands, since I could not talk anymore. And so I said I would not. I knew much more than they did about it. And then they put on my trail a man, a chemist, from the University of Delaware. He came to me representing a foundation in West Virginia, the Geschickter Foundation, and said that he wished to see these mushrooms and go down there to see how they worked. He said if I would take him along in my party he would help finance the trip. Well, that was rather important for us because these trips are a nuisance financially. I said, "All right we will take you along." And I took him along, though he was not a great success on the trip. This was written up later in a book on the CIA by John Marks (1980). He devotes a chapter to this episode in the CIA's history.[7]

RF: *A short while later you and Dr. Hofmann made another trip to Mexico, this time with the synthetic psilocybin capsules that Dr. Hofmann had made.*

RGW: Yes, that is right, in 1962.

RF: *Maria Sabina said that those capsules contained "the spirit of the mushroom" and that she would now be able to conduct the ritual when there were no mushrooms available.*

RGW: Yes, she contradicted herself somewhat. She was severe, and deservedly so, on the flow of visitors in her village; they did disgrace themselves, and they cheapened the whole performance. But then, on the other hand, she never ceased to like me and receive me and greet me as a friend.

RF: *Have you taken the synthetic psilocybin yourself?*

RGW: Yes, I have.

RF: *Was there a difference?*

RGW: I did not discover any difference. I think the people who discover a difference are looking for a difference, and they imagine they see a difference. But I am not an authority there. I do not pretend to be the last word.

RF: *Then after Mexico you turned your attention to the question of soma, the Vedic elixir of immortality.*

RGW: That's right.

RF: *Your book,* Soma: The Divine Mushroom of Immortality (1969), *argued convincingly to many leading scholars and Indologists that soma was the* Amanita muscaria (Smith 1972, 4).

RGW: Yes, but not all leading scholars. John Brough's review (Brough 1971), sent to me in thirty pages of congested type, which I have copies of here, was a severe one, but very polite. Of course for a layman to receive a review by Professor John Brough of Cambridge University in thirty pages of congested type was, in a way, a kind of compliment. I published my rejoinder to Brough a year later in 1971, in my series published by the Harvard Botanical Museum (Wasson 1971).

RF: *The journal that published Brough's review did not accept it?*

RGW: I did not expect them to accept it, and they did not accept it. They said they did not have space to. They only publish their own reviews, not rejoinders. And Professor Kuiper, a Dutchman, published a different review (Kuiper 1970). There were others.

RF: *I heard that you may have changed your mind about the* Amanita muscaria. *Is this still your position, that soma was the* Amanita muscaria *mushroom?*

RGW: Oh no! If you heard anything different, it was a mistake. Of course it was *Amanita muscaria,* and more we find that the *Amanita muscaria* was the sacred mushroom of the Maya—the Quiche Maya who left the *Popol Vuh.* The *calkulha* is the *Amanita muscaria,* the *calkulha* meaning—its primary meaning—is a terrific lightning bolt and the thunder that accompanies it. Can you think of a more powerful metaphor? It ennobles the mushroom sky high.

RF: *How does the Mayan mythology relate to the* Vedas?

RGW: Well, the two poems have at least two expressions that mean the same thing. The "one leg" is most important in those two poems. *Aja ekapad* in the Asian poem and *hurakan* in Quiche, they mean the same thing. They both mean *soma.* Both of them. There's no question about it. Some people could demur a little bit about *ekapad* being *soma,* but in

Quiche they talk about the *soma* and *hurakan* as the same word.

RF: *Do you think it is possible that there could have been more than one* soma? *There is another idea advanced by David Flattery at Berkeley that* soma *was* Peganum harmala.[8] *What do you think of this?*

RGW: Oh that is absurd, just absurd. That plant does not lead to a blissful state.

RF: *One might challenge your theory on these same grounds. Apparently the* Amanita muscaria *does not lead to a blissful state either.*

RGW: Well, I know. That troubles me too. I cannot explain it, but there must be some explanation. No white man enjoys a blissful experience that I know of from the *Amanita*. Now there are occasions.[9] We experimented in the *Amanita muscaria* season in October, two years running, in Japan, in the mountains north of Tokyo. Four of us, four mycologists, three of them Japanese, and myself who is not Japanese. We tried them three days running in two successive years—that is about six times—and we had no results whatever from them, except one, on the last day, and there was no mistaking his ecstasy. His state of mind was blissful. He was simply . . . We did not recognize him. He said, "This is so wonderful, this is really extraordinary. It is nothing like alcohol, alcohol is not in the same league." He spoke in Japanese, of course, but they translated it for me.

DH: *Was there anything different about that day or in the way the mushrooms were prepared?*

RGW: Well, the way it was prepared was each of us had a lamp, and we dried it. You see, it was in the season and in the season it was a fresh mushroom, and we knew it was made five times stronger by drying it. And since we were not there long enough to dry them on these successive days, we had these lamps. We held them up close to these lamps, but not close enough to cook it. Our hands could still stand the heat easily, and we dried it for twenty or thirty minutes until it was really a dried mushroom, but not burnt, not cooked. We were careful about that, and he was careful, too. What did he do that was different from the rest of us? We do not know if there was any difference, but he had a great experience. On the other hand, when he went home and told his wife about it, she made him promise never to do it again.

RF: *Have you had any correspondence with Mircea Eliade on this subject of mushrooms? He has never publicly responded to your work, critically or otherwise. Generally, his treatment of this subject has been rather weak and somewhat negative, although it has changed somewhat from his earliest writing in* Shamanism *(1964) and* Yoga: Immortality and Freedom *(1970), where, as you know, he refers to "intoxication by mushrooms" as "decadent," "late in derivation . . . ."* [10]

RGW: Yes. I wrote about that in *Soma*. Do you know that?

RF: *Yes, and did you know that in the first volume of* A History of Religious Ideas *he acknowledges the primary significance of soma in the development of all subsequent forms of Indian mysticism? He says that they all evolved to replace the absence of the original beverage (Eliade 1978). It is quite a different statement than he made in his earlier work. Have you had any communication with him?*

RGW: No, we have had no communication at all. Through Wendy I have asked about him and she has told me some things, but I have had no communication with him. He has not written me, and I have not written him.

RF: *I had a very interesting experience with him in June. He was my professor in Chicago. We had a number of conversations on sacred substances and the history of religion, and he always encouraged me to learn more about it. Finally I asked him if he would summarize his views because he had not really given the subject an adequate treatment, though it is central to all his other work. He finally agreed to an interview, and we arranged a time. When the time came, something quite unexpected happened. I remember our conversation word for word.*

When I arrived at his office he was looking quite disheveled and very tired.

Mircea Eliade: I cannot see you today.

RF: *Is something wrong, Professor?*

ME: I am in a depressed mood. I cannot think very well.

I thought if we just started the interview he might come out of it. So I said to him:

RF: *There are many people in the world who could benefit from learning your views on sacred plants.*

ME: Well, I cannot talk about it.

Really I was disappointed. I had worked hard preparing a good list of questions for him and looked forward to this being an important chapter in our book, so I said:

RF: *Professor, you have always been reluctant to address this issue and that surprises me because it is central to all your interests: alchemy, mythology, shamanism, yoga, contemporary secularization, religious studies methodology. . . . Once you said it was because it was such a controversial subject, but you have always been controversial.*

ME: Yes, I know. But I do not know anything about them.

This surprised me, too. I had just typed out twelve pages of quotations from just a few of his books pertaining to sacred plants or elixirs in the history of religion. I told him:

RF: *You didn't know anything about shamanism when you started studying that either.*

ME: Well, I am too old now. I cannot begin something new. Now please leave. I need to rest.

So I got up to leave, and as I stood up I said:

RF: *Tell me, professor, is it this subject, or something about this subject, that makes you feel so ill?*

ME: (waving his hands) Yes . . . no . . . well . . . yes! (then emphatically) I don't like these plants!

RGW: Really? He said that, "I don't like these plants"? Are you authorized to publish this interview with Eliade?

RF: *As I was leaving he asked me if I would be back in the autumn. I said I would, if he would be there, and when I suggested that we have the interview then he seemed to approve of the idea. I think he wants me to think about them more myself.*

RGW: How old is he?

RF: *Seventy-eight. He hasn't been well.* *He has very bad arthritis. His hands are all bandaged.*

RGW: That is awful.

RF: *He has acknowledged the possible significance of the matter. He mentions Aldous Huxley (Eliade 1977) indicating that there would be a great deal more to say on this subject, that they may be part of a solution to the problems of contemporary secularization.*

RGW: He never mentioned me.

RF: *Not to my knowledge, but he said in June that* The Road to Eleusis *(Wasson, Hofmann, and Ruck 1978) was on his summer reading list.*

DH: *What do you make of his reaction?*

RGW: Well, I think it is very interesting. He opens up the whole subject. It sounds to me as though he is admitting there is something he has overlooked.

RF: *Two weeks before our short interview at a reception honoring the*

---

*[Mircea Eliade passed away in April 1986. —Ed.]

establishment of the Mircea Eliade chair in the history of religion at the University of Chicago, one of his former students, in praise of his old professor, said to the gathering that Eliade once canceled his class so that students could go see a man who was speaking on campus about sacred, psychedelic plants. This was an example of how Eliade valued current topics and encouraged his students to explore wide-ranging issues.

RGW: Who was that?

RF: *Larry Sullivan was Eliade's student.* I have thought a lot about Eliade's reluctance to address this matter squarely, and I thought it may be due to an effort on his part to preserve the sacredness of these substances. Or maybe he has just inherited the Brahmanic aversion to these things in his early years as a yogi in India. Who knows? Maybe he was trying not to err in the way that you felt you erred, by exposing them outside of a sacred context. This is an interesting problem. In ancient Greece, for example, what you have done would have been punished by death. To divulge the secret of the Mysteries was strictly forbidden.*

RGW: By death yes, but there was always one exit. . . . In 415 B.C.E. there were shocking revelations of private sessions in the homes of various citizens in which the Eleusinian Mysteries were imitated. In what tone of voice they were imitated, whether they were made ridiculous or whether they were done respectfully, I don't know. No one knows, but they were imitated. Alkibiades was one of those people who did it, and he was summoned back from the commanding position he held at the siege of Syracuse and he fled to Sparta instead. And that was a big episode—a big episode![11]

RF: *This was your next great contribution, that is, your collaboration with Albert Hofmann and Carl Ruck on* The Road to Eleusis. *Your book shows that the mystical potion of the Mysteries, the* kykeon, *might well have been an entheogenic beverage derived from ergot, containing lysergic acid amides.*

---

*[Sullivan is presently professor of theology and anthropology at Notre Dame University. —Ed.]

RGW: Yes, that is right.

RF: *Has this book been reviewed?*

RGW: I have not seen it reviewed in any important event. I have seen it reviewed in newspapers. But they were just reports on the book; they were not really up to the job.

RF: *The book has not been critically reviewed by scholars?*

RGW: No. But it has been widely accepted.

RF: *If you are correct about the kykeon at Eleusis, there are profound implications regarding the foundation of our own society.*[12]

RGW: Of course, they would go to it only once. One person could go to it only once, and that produces a factor. Because of their amazement at the reaction, and that would be the end. They would not go back again and again as the Indians do in Mexico.

RF: *Have you ever tried to reproduce this kykeon?*

RGW: No.

RF: *Have you ever tried LSD?*

RGW: No.

RF: *There is a Titian painting, done in 1522–23, called* The Bacchanal. *Are you familiar with it?*

RGW: No, I am not.

RF: *Well, it is a very interesting painting. It depicts a Dionysian scene. There is a group of people that appear to be in a state of rapture. In the middle of the painting, there is a child, a little boy. He is pulling up his smock, and he is peeing into the river. Downstream from the boy, there is someone with a jug scooping up the river water. And this is poured into the celebrants' cups for drinking. There's a caption that reads, "He who drinks and drinks no more, doesn't know what drinking is" (Williams 1968, 90).*

RGW: I have not seen that painting, but I am delighted. It's called *The Bacchanal*? Well, there are several books out on Titian lately. I would like very much to see that painting. Where is it?

RF: *In the Prado. Your most recent investigation has been into the last meal of the Buddha (Wasson 1982). You say that Buddha's last meal may have been a plate of mushrooms called* putika *and that this helps to establish the identity of* soma.

RGW: I say it *was*. I do not say it *may* have been. It was the putika.

RF: *How does this help us to identify soma?*

RGW: Well, it helps us mightily in that it is a mushroom. That it is a mushroom is a strong argument in favor of soma being a mushroom (Wasson 1982). But we have so many evidences now of *Amanita muscaria* being soma that it is just an additional factor. When they talk about *aja ekapad,* "not born single foot." *Aja,* "not born"; why not born? "Not born" because there has been no seed. No seed. All plants and all animals, including mankind, spring from a seed. They knew that, and we know that. This says, "not born from seed." Now this means it belongs to the small element of growths that have no seed. Mushrooms are among the cryptogams. Cryptogams are the class that have no seed, and the mushrooms are the conspicuous element among the cryptogams. Well now, that is pretty conclusive. It was a mushroom. We have many other evidences of it.

RF: *I have always wondered how your banking colleagues reacted to your adventures with the mushrooms.*

RGW: Well, they were very interested in it. No other bank in New York would have allowed it, but, well, they did not know anything about what I was doing when I was going down to Mexico until my article appeared in *Life,* and then it got to be known. I asked Henry Alexander, the head of the bank, if there would be any objection, and he said there would be no objection. I was relieved for I did not wish to leave the bank.

RF: *Do you think that you would have at that point?*

RGW: Oh yes, I would have.

RF: *By now you felt you were on the trail of something quite profound.*

RGW: Yes, exactly.

RF: *I wanted to ask you another question about Maria Sabina. In a book about her life (Estrada 1981), Maria Sabina says that before you, nobody took the mushrooms only to find God. They were always taken for the sick to get well, or news of an absent loved one, or other such reasons.*

RGW: Who did the translation?

RF: *Henry Munn translated it into English.*

RGW: But Henry Munn doesn't know Mazatec.

RF: *He did the translation from Spanish into English. From Mazatec to Spanish was done by Alvaro Estrada.*

RGW: Oh yes, Alvaro Estrada took down her life in Mazatec. He is a Mazatec Indian, and it is a marvelous book. I do not like the English translation. Henry Munn was brought up in this country and went to Bowdoin College, then went off the deep end, traveled and traveled, and wrote a million words—more than a million words—on his experiences with entheogens. He is so wordy.

RF: *He is a storyteller. You think this was a bad translation?*

RGW: Yes. That does not sound at all like Maria Sabina.

RF: *When you read her story in that book, you can see what hardships she went through. There was a lot of violence in her life and many problems with alcohol where she lived.*

RGW: Yes. Well, her son was murdered, and one of her husbands beat her unmercifully. The other one was a restless old drunkard. When we first visited her, she was recovering from a pistol wound. Yet she went through it all. She was a shaman.

DH: *What's that old saying? "Some husbands lead their wives to the path, and some drive them there."*

RF: *How she could have managed to perform her duties as a* curandera *under such difficult conditions. . . ?*

RGW: As a *sabia.* As they explain in their book, there are three levels. The bottom level is *brujo,* which she mentions with approbation. *Brujo* is the lowest level, which means you do not need to know very much. There is the *curandera* level. And then there was the *sabia* level. *Sabia,* from the root *sabe.* So she was the wise woman.

DH: *Now if I understood you correctly, you were saying that one is born into these different levels according to the "antiquity of one's soul" or one's innate level of understanding?*

RGW: Yes, that is right. You are born into these different levels. Of course, that is the same as India.

RF: *You were saying before that Henry Alexander, the chief of the bank, was very enthusiastic about this.*

RGW: Yes, and that, of course, cleared the way for the whole institution.

RF: *Were any of your banking colleagues ever enthusiastic enough to try the mushrooms with you?*

RGW: No, none. I did not associate them with any of my investigations into the mushrooms. None. I did not try to. At lunch they would ask me. They would try to draw me out, inquiring about my experiences in Mexico. But I was talking about banking.

RF: *Why didn't you want to talk about it?*

RGW: I did not wish to get involved trying to educate people who were totally ignorant of the subject. Anyway, I did not. I may have been wrong. Perhaps I should have started to convert everyone. It may have been the source of a revolution on Wall Street!

RF: *Many of us have had that fantasy—turning on the financial world to entheogenic experiences—so I wanted to ask you how your mushroom experiences changed your worldview.*

RGW: Heaven knows? How it changed my worldview? I will have to get somebody to tell you what my worldview was before and what my worldview is now. I do not know what my worldview is now if you asked me.

RF: *Bankers generally have quite different outlooks than those who explore entheogens. Usually they are more materialistic, secular, and so on, whereas with entheogens you'll find a different sort. The people and the cultures that use them tend to have a different achievement motive.*

RGW: You may be right. But I do not concern myself with those questions. I just go about my inquiries on my own.

RF: *Have your mushroom experiences affected how you think about the afterlife?*

RGW: No. Not at all. They have had no bearing on it.

RF: *You mention in* The Road to Eleusis *that these experiences can help us understand Plato's ideas regarding the world of forms, the ideal world. . . .*

RGW: Plato had taken the kykeon at Eleusis and had the experience. He saw those forms—"ideas" he called them—in another world, and he said that everything had an archetype somewhere in a different sphere. I think he took this from his experience at Eleusis, but he could not say so. It would be illegal to reveal the secrets. And yet, the priestesses there could not advance charges against him without their being the source of public knowledge of their Mysteries.

RF: *A lot of people who are interested in this subject think it is of great* *importance to revitalize religion by renewing a sense of the sacred in our society. What are your feelings about this?*

RGW: I do not like to deal with such immense subjects. I have my own thoughts, but they are not really worth repeating. I do not like to discuss them.[13]

DH: *What do you think the significance of your rediscovery of the mushroom is? Its importance in religion? What significance do you think it has for the culture, or could have?*

RGW: Oh my, that's another big question. You two are capable of handling, of dancing with these . . . but I am incapable of thinking in these important trends in world thought. I just plug away at it and let the chips fall where they may. I am ashamed to admit to you that I don't deal in these things with a magisterial manner, like the conductor of an orchestra. I don't do that.

RF: *Would you comment on John Allegro's work (1970) regarding the origins of Christianity?*

RGW: I think John Allegro was a brilliant man. He was of Jewish origin, an Italian Jew. Then he went up to live in England. At Oxford, he was leader in the linguistic circle and was a most promising linguist, and the result was that he was appointed to the panel that investigated the Dead Sea Scrolls as England's representative—or as Great Britain's representative. That was a great big honor and a deserved honor. He wrote one the first books on the Dead Sea Scrolls (Allegro 1956). It sold more than a million copies but is already outdated by other books. It is solid work and is to be esteemed. Then he took a post at Manchester University.

I heard of him first through friends in Sweden who wrote me asking, "Who is this man, Allegro, writing about mushrooms? He never mentions you, but he is writing about mushrooms, and he is asking us questions about mushrooms." And I didn't know it at that time, but he was someone who was working, Allegro, his name was, and he hadn't had any publicity at all. Then along came his book, *The Sacred Mushroom and the Cross,* and he made the unforgivable blunder of selling the manuscript to *The News of the World*! *The News of the World* is the disreputable sheet that comes out only on Sunday in Britain. It is like the *National Enquirer* is here—a disreputable sheet! He sold it to them for thirty thousand pounds, when pounds were worth more than they are today. He sold it to them, and they came out week after week, with extracts from this manuscript, eight column headlines on the front page, "Jesus Only a Penis!"

His colleagues at Manchester they just . . . Although they have the security of tenure in England at the universities, this they could not bear. They had to get rid of him. So he retired to the Isle of Man, a rural island. It is a very lovely island. I would love to spend the rest of my days there. It is just as lovely as this is here. They speak Manx. Manx is a Gaelic language, as is Irish, Welsh, and Gaelic in Scotland. There are only a few hundred people there. Anyway, I had his address and wrote him a letter after he had gone out there and said, "I should like to correspond with you, if you will correspond." I never heard from him.

RF: *Could you comment on his book?*

RGW: Well, of course, I think he jumped to unwarranted conclusions on scanty evidence. And when you make such blunders as attributing the Hebrew language, the Greek language, to Sumerian, that is unacceptable to any linguist. The Sumerian language is a parent to no language, and no one knows where it came from. It was spoken at the mouth of the Euphrates around the gulf of Persia. It was spoken there, and it became an official language of record; documents were kept in that language, written in cuneiform for a long time. In the Akkadian culture for some centuries it was like writing Latin in England during the Middle Ages as the official language. But as far as being a parent to Hebrew and Greek, that is incredible.

RF: *And didn't he speak about the record of the mushroom in Egypt?*

RGW: I think he did. But no one knows what word was used in Egypt for the mushroom. There are lots of botanical words in ancient Egyptian that have never been identified, and perhaps it is in among those words. It probably is among those words, because there are mushrooms in the Nile delta, in season, many mushrooms.

RF: *What are your feelings about what happened in the 1960s in this culture with regard to the youths' and the media's treatment of psychedelics?*

RGW: Well, I did not feel very good about it, and I did not approve of it.

RF: *Were you at all involved in the research at Harvard with Timothy Leary?*

RGW: Oh, no, I was not! Timothy Leary came down to New York with his friend Alpert and called on me at One East End Avenue and urged me—to the extent of his ability—to join them both and be on their board of directors when they were starting a new religion up at Millbrook.

RF: *That was the League for Spiritual Discovery?*

RGW: Yes, I think so. Well, I declined, absolutely declined to be with them! Oh, I could not have done anything else. I do not congratulate myself on my decision, because Timothy Leary was a . . . I hate to go on record as saying this, but I can say I consider him an egoist of the first class. And he wished to get me. He would have made a great show of me, an exhibit, but I would only be the object of attention. I would not have anything to say. Oh my, it would have been a mistake. I thought so at the time, and I think so still. Timothy Leary and Alpert—who is now Ram Dass. Where is he now?

RF: *He travels frequently representing the Hanuman Foundation, raising consciousness about spirituality and modern life. He works often with dying patients, teaching meditation. . . .*

RGW: Do you have to do or go through all that to die properly? I don't think so.

RF: *Well, I don't know, but I think these methods that come from the East represent something different to the ones who are suffering, and the freshness of it captures their attention. In the West we've ignored these questions of dying.*

RGW: Does he run the place?

RF: *I'm not sure if he runs it, but he is an important part of it.*

RGW: What is Tim Leary doing?

DH: *You will not believe this. He's into computers.*

RGW: He's turned into a computer?

DH: *No, not yet. But that might eventually be one of his goals. I wouldn't mind having Tim's intelligence in my computer someday. He is currently designing what he calls "psychoactive software," which are mind-expanding, interactive games that are based on his work in psychometrics. His latest game, Mind Mirror, utilizes role-playing and intriguing scenarios to teach people social skills and empathy. In addition to being a powerful psychological tool, the game is exciting and fun to play.*

RF: *I've heard him say computers will be the "acid of the eighties."*

DH: *Then Dick Price (cofounder of Esalen Institute) said, "Tim will be the first person to get computers made illegal!" At any rate, his work is extremely interesting and much more accessible than when he was in his space migration period.*

RGW: Space migration? That's what I expected him to be doing.*

RF: *Since we mentioned space migration, I wanted to say that entheogens, and particularly mushrooms, have this interesting property of linking us up, in a kind of telepathic or some other mysterious way, with extraordinary,*

---

*[Timothy Leary passed away on May 31, 1996. —Ed.]

other dimensional levels of reality—as if they are a way for humans to engage a higher level of consciousness. It is the ultimate humility to admit that this higher intelligence comes somehow through an interaction with a mushroom, I know, but so many people report experiences of exactly this and have for millennia. Many people say they have felt in contact with an awesome religious force that spans the universe—a kind of fibrous web of energy and intelligence—when they have taken the mushrooms in a respectful way. What do you think of that?

RGW: I am afraid that since I am alone working here I do not have the contacts that you have. I do not know anything about what they are thinking, but I don't think I have had that impression when I have taken the mushroom. Now I have not taken them for many years. It is not a fair thing to take, I find, every Saturday night. And I do not deal with those questions.

RF: *What would you say your main contribution is in this field?*

RGW: Well, my main contribution, I have to say, are those books on that shelf there. And in those books I deal at length with many of the questions you are asking.

DH: *I wish they weren't all out of print.*

RGW: Well, have you *The Wondrous Mushroom* (Wasson 1980)? I may have a copy here I can give you. That is a good book—*The Wondrous Mushroom*. In fact they are all good books—says the author.

RF: *Mr. Wasson, you say that you are not orchestrating this grand scheme. Who, or what, do you believe is?*

RGW: Who is?

RF: *Or what is? Do you see these mushrooms as some sort of evolutionary agents?*

RGW: I think they are quite primitive. They go back very far. There are more entheogens than we suspect. Now we are finding more and more.

RF: *How do you think your discoveries can benefit society?*

RGW: These are big questions. I prefer to not answer that question.

RF: *Could you point in some direction for future work in the field? What would you like to explore? The story of Adam and Eve seems to be a likely mythology to explore for its possible entheogenic significance.*

RGW: Have you read the passage on that in this coming book (*Persephone's Quest: Entheogens and the Origins of Religion,* Wasson 1987)? I will give you that. Here, if you will read this:

RF: *This is from the first chapter of* Persephone's Quest, *section sixteen, "The Tree of the Knowledge of Good and Evil." You write:*

I once said that there was no mushroom in the Bible. I was wrong. It plays a hidden role (that is, hidden from us until now) and a major one, in what is the best known episode in the Old Testament, the Garden of Eden story and what happened to Adam and Eve.

I suppose that few at first, or perhaps none, will agree with me. To propose a novel reading of this celebrated story is a daring thing: it is exhilarating and intimidating. I am confident, ready for the storm. I hold that the tree of the knowledge of good and evil was *soma,* was the *calkuhla* was *Amanita muscaria,* the Nameless Mushroom of the English-speaking people. The tree was probably a conifer, in Mesopotamia. The serpent, being underground, was the faithful attendant on the fruit. (See my *Soma,* 214). Please read the Biblical story in light of all I have written on the awe and reverence that *Amanita muscaria* evokes, and how the knowing ones speak of it only when alone together, preferably by night. Gradually it will dawn on you that the "fruit" can be no other than soma. Everyone mentions the tree but its fruit is nameless. There were two trees in the Bible story, the Tree of the Knowledge of Good and Evil, whose fruit Adam and Eve were forbidden to eat, and the Tree of Life. Adam and Eve ate of the fruit of the Tree of the Knowledge of Good and Evil, but they were expelled from the Garden to prevent them from eating of the Tree of Life, which would have conferred immortality on them.

RGW: Now please read the following text, from the American revision—Genesis chapters 2 and 3:

Chap. 2:9: And out of the ground made Jehovah God to grow every tree that is pleasant to the sight, and good for food; the tree of life also in the midst of the garden, and the tree of the knowledge of good and evil. . . . 16. And Jehovah God commanded the man, saying, of every tree in the garden thou mayest freely eat; 17. but of the tree of knowledge of good and evil, thou shalt not eat of it, for in the day that thou eat thereof thou shalt surely die. . . . 25. And they were both naked, the man and his wife, and were not ashamed.

Chap. 3:1–13: Now the serpent was more subtle than any beast of the field which Jehovah God had made. And he said unto the woman, Yea, hath God said, Ye shall not eat of any tree of the garden? And the woman said unto the serpent, Of the fruit of the trees of the garden we may eat: but of the fruit of the tree which is in the midst of the garden, God hath said, Ye shall not eat of it, neither shall ye touch it, lest ye die. And the serpent said unto the woman, Ye shall not surely die: for God doth know that in the day ye eat thereof, then your eyes shall be opened, and ye shall be as God, knowing good and evil. And when the woman saw that the tree was good for food, and that it was a delight to the eyes, and that the tree was to be desired to make one wise, she took of the fruit thereof and did eat: and she gave also unto her husband with her, and he did eat. And the eyes of both of them were opened, and they knew that they were naked; and they sewed fig leaves together, and they made themselves aprons. . . .

Therefore Jehovah God inflicted the penalties for their disobedience: on the serpent, he was to go for evermore on his belly; on Eve, she would suffer the pangs of childbirth; on Adam, he would undergo a lifetime of drudgery. We continue quoting from the text:

Chap. 3:22–24: And Jehovah God said, Behold, the man is become as one of us, to know good and evil; and now, lest he put forth his hand, and take also of the tree of life, and eat, and live for ever— therefore Jehovah God sent him forth from the Garden of Eden, to till the ground from whence he was taken. So he drove out the man; and he placed at the east of the garden of Eden the Cherubim, and the flame of a sword which turned every way, to keep the way of the tree of life.

Adam and Eve became self-conscious from eating the "fruit" and wove fig leaves into aprons to cover themselves from each other and from Jehovah God.

RGW: They became "self-conscious." That is the thing that distinguishes humanity from all other species, "self-consciousness."

RF: *Yes, this is an important element in the McKennas' theory also. This is the evolutionary leap, part of the evolutionary leap. . . . You continue writing:*

The story carries the mystical resonance of the early days, in Mesopotamia, where grew cedars and other conifers.

Some months ago I read the Garden of Eden tale once more, after not having thought of it since childhood. I read it as one who now knew the entheogens. Right away it came over me that the Tree of Knowledge was the tree that has been revered by many tribes of early man in Eurasia precisely because there grows under it the mushroom, splendid to look at, that supplies the entheogenic food to which early man attributed miraculous powers. He who composed the tale for us in Genesis was clearly steeped in the lore of this entheogen: he refrained from identifying the "fruit": he was writing for the initiates who would recognize what he was speaking about. I was an initiate. Strangers and also the unworthy would remain in the dark. Adam and Eve had eaten the "fruit," being led to do so by the serpent, the faithful attendant on the "fruit," what the mycologists call *Amanita muscaria,* what the initiates call by a variety of euphemisms, which change from time to time, and we have seen to what strange lengths the uninitiated go when these euphemisms are detached from the "fruit" that they represent. The priestly redactor who set down the Genesis tale, an initiate and a believer, attributed to the "fruit" the gift of self-consciousness, a remarkable observation because self-consciousness is one of the major traits that distinguish humankind from all the other creatures. Is it not surprising that the composer of the story gave credit for this particular gift to our mushroom? It is unlikely that he was alone in doing so.

RF: *Yes, very interesting, and it fits in with what the McKennas are saying. But it is not the* A. muscaria, *which impresses them so much; it is* the Stropharia cubensis, *as we have said. They, too, are putting forth the idea that these mushrooms may not only be responsible for the genesis of religion, as you have suggested before (Wasson 1957; Wasson, Hofmann, Ruck 1978), but also for the genesis of the consciousness that distinguishes us from the other primates, as you are saying now (McKenna 1991).*

Some of the oldest cave art found, the Tassili frescoes, clearly depict shamanic use of mushrooms five to eight thousand years ago in Africa in a culture that is still a mystery to us (Lhote 1959). The McKennas are saying that perhaps the mushrooms stimulated this activity of the brain and gave us access to speech and accelerated our symbol-forming capacities. It is our consciousness that distinguishes us from other animals, and this is what is most radically affected by the entheogens.

Dennis McKenna suggested I ask you about the Paracus tapestries from Peru. Do you know them?

RGW: Yes I do. The authorities on those tapestries do not believe it is a mushroom they are representing. Well, I believe they may be wrong. I am not versed well enough in the histories of those tapestries to say so. I do not wish to get out on the end of a limb. But they seem quite dogmatic. They think they know what those signs mean. I forget who my authority—a consultant at Harvard—was.

RF: *Marlene Dobkin de Rios, in her recent book* Hallucinogens: Cross

Cultural Perspectives *(1984), says it pictures a person with a hammer, though the shape of it does not quite look like a hammer. The color scheme is exactly that of the* Amanita.

RGW: I have some beautiful photographs of those tapestries at my library at Harvard.[14] It could well be a mushroom, but I forget what explanation they gave me. I did not care to rejoin them. I have always been afraid of being too inclusive in my statements—that I accept anything shaped as a mushroom as being a mushroom.

RF: *You mentioned in* The Road to Eleusis *where an old friend congratulated you on your work in Mexico, but said, "May I offer you a word of warning? Stick to your Mexican mushroom cult and beware of seeing mushrooms everywhere"* (Wasson, Hofmann, Ruck 1978).

RGW: Well, I have the backing of Carl Ruck, a professor of classics at Boston University.

RF: *And also Robert Graves.*

RGW: But Robert Graves still felt it was *Amanita muscaria* at Eleusis, and there I disagree with him flatly! It was ergot—the parasite on the barley plant, on the wheat plant.[15]

RF: *There is a great difference experientially between the* Amanita muscaria *and lysergic acid amide. . . .*

RGW: Well, there are different chemicals appearing in the different mushrooms. The chemical in *Amanita muscaria* is utterly different from the chemicals appearing in *Psilocybes* and in ergot, which are related to each other. They are now in the process of discovering a plant in Mexico. . . . I cannot remember the name. I am getting tired now. We'd better stop.

RF: *Is there anything we did not ask that you would like to answer?*

RGW: Your questions were very good, intelligent, both of you.

DH: *Is there anything we have missed?*

RGW: Oh my, let's talk more later. Thank you both very much.

RF: *Thank you very much.*

NOTES

1. Robert Graves, late poet and classicist, author of many books of poetry, mythology, and culture, had long been interested in mushrooms and religion. His view is most concisely expressed in his essay "Centaur's Food," appearing in his collection *Food for Centaurs;* cf. his introduction to *The Sufis* by Idries Shah.

2. Peter Stafford (1992, 229) points out that religious intoxicants were in Wasson's blood long before the mushroom quest: "R. Gordon Wasson is the American son of an Episcopal minister who had written *Religion and Drink,* a book that examined biblical references to the drinking of alcohol by religious figures. He took the tack of a fundamentalist, which he was not, and implied that it would be quite unchristian to be critical of alcohol. The royalties of this book enabled the younger Wasson to study in Spain."

3. Daniel H. H. Ingalls, one of the world's leading Sanskrit scholars and professor emeritus at Harvard University, later favorably reviewed Wasson's soma hypothesis (Ingalls 1971a, 1971b).

4. "Not once does Maria Sabina reproach me for having made known to the world both the mushrooms and her gift as their ministrant. But not without anguish do I read her words:

   Before Wasson I felt that the holy children elevated me. I don't feel like that anymore. The force has diminished. If Cayetano hadn't brought the foreigners . . . the holy children would not have lost their power. . . . From the moment the foreigners arrived the holy children lost their purity. They lost their force; the foreigners spoiled them. From now on they won't be any good. There's no remedy for it.

   "These words make me wince: I, Gordon Wasson, am held responsible for the end of a religious practice in Mesoamerica that goes back far, for a millennium. I fear she spoke the truth, exemplifying her wisdom. A practice that had been carried on in secret for centuries has now been aerated, and aeration spells the end" (Estrada 1981, 19–20).

5. Richard Evans Schultes retired in June 1985 from a distinguished career as

professor in the natural sciences, director and curator of economic botany, Botanical Museum of Harvard University. He has authored numerous scientific articles on the botany and biochemistry of medicinal and psychoactive plants in addition to several books (see references). For many decades Dr. Schultes used the participant-observer method in his field research. Although he has consumed many of the substances of which he writes in the line of duty, he claims to never have had a "mystical experience" from any of them. One time he said he "felt like dancing" after such an experiment, and a longtime student of his remarked, "For Dr. Schultes to feel like dancing means that was a mystical experience."

6. Albert Hofmann was retired from his position as head of the Pharmaceutical-Chemical Research Laboratories, Division of Natural Products, Sandoz, Ltd., Basel, Switzerland. In addition to his well-known contributions to psychedelic knowledge, he has also discovered the important medicines hydergine, used to combat senility; methergine, for postpartum bleeding; and oxytocic ergonovine, for stimulating birth. For a full account of his illustrious career in chemistry, health, philosophy, and religion see Hofmann 1983, 1989.

7. John Marks (1980, 114–5) writes:

> *Joining Moore and Wasson on the 1956 trip were the world renowned French mycologist Roger Heim and a colleague from the Sorbonne. The party made the final leg of the trip, one at a time, in a tiny Cessna, but when it was Moore's turn, the load proved too much for the plane. The pilot suddenly took a dramatic right angle turn through a narrow canyon and made an unscheduled stop on the side of a hill. . . . The pilot decided to lighten the load by leaving Moore among the local Indians who spoke neither English or Spanish. Later in the day the pilot returned and picked up the shaken Moore.*
>
> *Finally in Huatla, sleeping on a dirt floor and eating local food, everyone reveled in the primitiveness of the adventure except Moore, who suffered. In addition to diarrhea, he recalls, "I had a terribly bad cold, we damn near starved to death, and I itched all over." Beyond his physical woes, Moore became more and more alienated recalls Wasson. "He was like a landlubber at sea. He got sick to his stomach and hated it all." Moore states, "Our relationship deteriorated during the course of the trip."*
>
> *Wasson returned to Maria Sabina who had led him to the high*

ground the year before. Again the ritual started well after dark and, for everyone but Moore, it was an enchanted evening. Sings Wasson: "I had the most superb feeling—a feeling of ecstasy. You're raised to a height where you have not been in everyday life—not ever." Moore, on the other hand, never left the lowlands. His description: "There was all this chanting in the dialect. Then they passed the mushrooms around, and we chewed them up. I did feel the hallucinogenic effect, although 'disoriented' would be a better word to describe my reaction."

8. Professor Flattery's work, coauthored with M. Schwartz, has since been published: "Haoma and Harmaline: The Botanical Identity of the Indo-Iranian Sacred hallucinogen 'Soma' and Its Legacy in Religion, Language, and Middle Eastern Folklore." University of California Publications Near Eastern Studies, (21) (1988).

9. Since this conversation with Mr. Wasson, Forte met Clark Heinrich, an independent scholar and mycophile who was inspired by Mr. Wasson's writings to embark upon a lengthy, courageous experiment with the *Amanita muscaria,* culminating, after many attempts, in a profound religious rapture, much like descriptions in the *Rig Veda.* The experience awakened in Heinrich a sense of how *A. muscaria* may be disguised in other religious writings including the Old and New Testaments and those associated with Gnosticism and alchemy. Heinrich has since composed his speculations into a book, *Magic Mushrooms in Religion and Alchemy* (2005).

10. Mircea Eliade, Sewell L. Avery distinguished service professor emeritus, University of Chicago, passed away in the spring of 1986. He was seventy-eight. Through his work he lives on as one of the foremost authorities of the history of religion, having written definitively on yoga, shamanism, mythology, and alchemy in over thirty scholarly books, and the history of religion generally in a monumental three-volume set, *A History of Religious Ideas* (1978, 1981, 1985). His earliest reporting on sacred plants is brief, somewhat naive, and distinctly negative. Wasson summarizes and critiques his position in *Soma* (1969, 326–34). In his later work Eliade (1978, 212) states the following:

We will not stop to consider the surrogates and substitutes for the original plant in the cult. It is the role that these somic experiences play in Indian thought that is important. Very probably such experiences were confined to priests and a certain number of sacrificers. But they had considerable repercussions by virtue of the hymns that praised them and especially by virtue of the interpretations the hymns called forth. The revelation of a full and beatific existence, in communion with the gods, continued to haunt Indian spirituality long after the disappearance of the original drink. Hence an attempt was made to attain such an existence by the help of other means: asceticism or orgiastic excesses, meditation, the techniques of Yoga, mystical devotion. . . . . In addition, the quest for absolute freedom gave rise to a whole series of methods and philosophoumena that, in the last analysis, opened out into new perspectives and vistas, unsuspected in the Vedic period. In all these later developments, the god Soma played not a very prominent role; it is the cosmological and sacrificial principle that he signified which ended by preempting the attention of theologians and metaphysicians.

11. George Mylonas writes:

   When Alkibiades, in a drunken state, dared to imitate acts of the celebration, he was condemned in absentia, his property was confiscated, all the priests and priestesses of the state were called upon to pronounce curses upon him. . . . It will perhaps be interesting to read again the accusation against as given by Plutarch: "Thessalos, son of Kimon, of the deme of Lakiadai, impeaches Alkibiades, son of Kleinas, of the deme of Skambonidai, for committing crime against the Goddess of Eleusis, Demeter, and Kore, by imitating the mysteries and showing them forth to his own companions in his own house, wearing a robe such as the Hierophant wears when he shows forth the sacred secrets to the initiates, and calling himself Hierophant and hailing the rest of his companions as Mystai and Epoptai, contrary to the laws and institutions of the Eumolpids, Kerykes, and priests of Eleusis" (Mylonas 1961, 224).

12. *Though Athens brought forth numerous divine things, yet she never created anything nobler than those sublime Mysteries through which we became gentler and have advanced from a barbarous and rustic life to a more civilized one, so that we not only live more joyfully but also die with a better hope (Cicero De Legibus 1:14).*

13. *We have suggested that divine mushrooms played a vital part in shaking loose early man's imagination, in arousing his capacity for self-perception, for awe, wonder, and reverence. They certainly made it easier for him to entertain the idea of God. . . .*

   Here is a sense in which the kingdom of God is within us; and the music of spheres turns out to be a physiological symphony. Let not this reflection disturb the believer in a Supreme Architect, for the ultimate enigma always remains close by, and man's most searching inquiries are always confined within the dark bound of the flexible but impenetrable envelope of the unknown, of that dark, distensible womb that is our prison and our Eden (Wasson and Wasson 1957, 375–76).

14. Two years later I visited the Wasson Library at Harvard to view these photographs and discovered in one an ambiguous object in the hand of a creature who appears to be flying. It could be a mushroom or a hammer. At the same time I found that the Boston Museum of Fine Arts has stored in their basement several of the original tapestries. These tapestries were woven by the Nazca people of ancient Peru, the makers of the famous Nazca lines, around 700 B.C.E. The Nazca lines are elaborate and immense designs on the ground that are intelligible only from considerable heights, leading some to speculate that the Nazca people had some contact with folks in flying machines. The tapestries were burial mantles, used to wrap corpses for funerals. One of these wraps depicts a creature holding lightly in his or her fingers a delicate mushroom (certainly not a hammer), and his or her eyes are exactly cross-sections of a mushroom cap and stipe. Could it be that the Nazca people knew the mushroom to be an avenue to the world of the departed? Is it possible that they understood ecstatic travel? Could they fly out of their body while bemushroomed? Maybe they didn't need flying machines at all to view their art. Recall that in the Yoga Sutras (4:1) Patanjali lists magic herbs as one of the possible means to develop *siddhis* (powers), among them, "flying."

15. Robert Graves (1961, 281–82) writes:

> *To me it is reasonably clear—though I have not yet examined the bas-relief itself—that the sculptor was blabbing a secret: "Fly amanite is the source of prophetic inspiration at Eleusis." Gordon Wasson hopes that I may be right—for mycophobic Classical scholars seem to be in the habit of calling mushrooms "flowers"—but he, being more cautious than I, hesitates to commit himself to a point of such importance, until he has taken expert advise. He also tells me that Greek vase-experts usually describe Nessus's mushrooms as "wading birds." Yet no Greek wading bird has a silhouette like a panaelous mushroom and Greek vase-painters keep a proportion of the animals fairly exact. . . . I have now visited the Metropolitan Museum to check up, and if those are wading birds, then I am a Centaur; but the Museum authorities insist that they are. . . . Also that the mushroom in the Pharsalus*

Relief is a rose; or alternatively, the knucklebone of a sheep.

All right, all right! Disregard the flower (or knucklebone, big enough for an elephant's) in the foreground! Observe the pretty wading birds! And whatever else you do, don't introduce any sort of toadstool into our serene Classical atmosphere!

REFERENCES

Allegro, J. *People of the Dead Sea Scrolls.* New York: Pelican Books, 1956.

———. *The Sacred Mushroom and the Cross.* New York: Doubleday, 1970.

Brough, J. "Soma and *Amanita Muscaria.*" *Bulletin of the School of Oriental and African Studies* 34 (2) (1971).

Cicero *De Legibus* 1:14.

Dobkin de Rios, M. D. *Hallucinogens: Cross Cultural Perspectives.* Albuquerque, N.M.: University of New Mexico Press, 1984.

Eliade, M. *Shamanism: Archaic Techniques of Ecstasy.* Princeton, N.J.: Bollingen Series, 1964.

———. *Yoga: Immortality and Freedom.* Princeton, N.J.: Bollingen Series, 1970.

———. *No Souvenirs.* New York: Harper and Row, 1977.

———. *A History of Religious Ideas,* vols. 1–3. Chicago: University of Chicago Press, 1978, 1981, 1985.

Estrada, A. *Maria Sabina: Her Life and Chants.* Santa Barbara, Calif.: Ross-Erikson, 1981.

Flattery, D., and M. Schwartz. "Haoma and Harmaline: The Botanical Identity of the Indo-Iranian Sacred Hallucinogen 'Soma' and Its Legacy in Religion, Language, and Middle Eastern Folklore." University of California Publications Near Eastern Studies (21) (1988).

Graves, R. *Food for Centaurs.* New York: Doubleday, 1961.

Heim, R., and R. Wasson. *Les Champignons Hallucinogenes du Mexico.* Paris: Editions du Museum National d'Histoire Naturelle, 1958.

Heinrich, C. *Strange Fruit.* London: Bloomsbury, 1995.

Hofmann, A. *LSD: My Problem Child.* Los Angeles: J. P. Tarcher, 1983.

———. *Insight Outlook.* Atlanta, Ga.: Humanics New Age, 1989.

Ingalls, D. H. H. "Remarks on Mr. Wasson's *Soma.*" *Journal of the American Oriental Society* 91 (2) (1971a): 188–91.

———. Review of *Soma,* by R. G. Wasson. *The New York Times Book Review,* September 5, 1971, 15.

Kuiper, F. "Review of Wasson 1968." *Indo-Iranian Journal* 12 (4) (1970): 279–85.

Lhote, H. *The Search for the Tassilli Frescoes.* New York: Dutton, 1959.

Marks, J. *The Search for "The Manchurian Candidate."* New York: McGraw-Hill, 1980.

McKenna, T. *The Archaic Revival.* San Francisco: HarperCollins, 1991.

———. *Food of the Gods.* New York: Bantam, 1992.

———. *True Hallucinations.* San Francisco: HarperCollins, 1993.

McKenna, D., and T. McKenna. *The Invisible Landscape.* San Francisco: HarperCollins, 1994.

Mylonas, G. *Eleusis and the Eleusinian Mysteries.* Princeton, N.J.: Princeton University Press, 1961.

Riedlinger, T. *The Sacred Mushroom Seeker.* Portland, Ore.: Dioscorides Press, 1990.

Ruck, C. A. P., et al. "Entheogens." *Journal of Psychedelic Drugs* 11 (1–2) (1979): 145–46.

Schultes, R. "Plantae Mexicanae II: The Identification of Teonanacatl." *Botanical Museum Leaflets* 7. Cambridge, Mass.: Harvard University, 1939.

———. "Teonanacatl: The Narcotic Mushroom of the Aztecs." *American Anthropologist* 42 (1940): 429–43.

———. *Hallucinogenic Plants.* New York: Golden Books, 1976.

Schultes, R., and A. Hofmann. *The Botany and Chemistry of Hallucinogens.* Springfield, Ohio: Charles C. Thomas, 1980.

———. *Plants of the Gods.* Rochester, Vt.: Healing Arts Press, 1992.

Smith, H. "Wasson's Soma: A Review Article." *Journal of the American Academy of Religion* 40 (1972).

Stafford, P. *Psychedelics Encyclopedia.* Berkeley, Calif.: Ronin Publishing, 1992.

Tedlock, D. *Popul Vuh.* New York: Simon and Schuster, 1985.

Wasson, R. "Seeking the Magic Mushroom." *Life,* May 17, 1957, 100–20.

———. *Soma: Divine Mushroom of Immortality.* New York: Harcourt Brace Jovanovich, 1969.

———. "Inquiry into the Origin of the Religious Idea among Primitive People." *Botanical Museum Leaflets* 19 (7). Cambridge, Mass.: Harvard University, 1971.

———. *The Wondrous Mushroom.* New York: McGraw-Hill, 1980.

———. "The Last Meal of the Buddha." *Journal of the American Oriental Society* 102 (4) (1982): 591–603.

———. *Persephone's Quest: Entheogens and the Origins of Religion.* New Haven, Conn.: Yale University Press, 1987.

Wasson, R., G. Cowan, F. Cowan, and W. Rhodes. *Maria Sabina and Her Mazatec Mushroom Velada.* New York: Harcourt Brace Jovanovich, 1974.

Wasson, R., A. Hofmann, and C. Ruck. *The Road to Eleusis.* New York: Harcourt Brace Jovanovich, 1978.

Wasson, R., and V. Wasson. *Mushrooms, Russia and History.* New York: Pantheon, 1957.

Williams, J. *The World of Titian.* New York: Time, 1968.

9 SACRED MUSHROOM PENTECOST

Thomas J. Riedlinger

Thomas J. Riedlinger is a writer and lecturer. A fellow of the Linnean Society of London, he earned his undergraduate degree in psychology from Northwestern University and his master's degree in world religions from Harvard Divinity School. His published works include *The Sacred Mushroom Seeker: Essays for R. Gordon Wasson* and articles appearing in the *Journal of Humanistic Psychology,* the *Journal of Psychoactive Drugs,* the *Journal of Transpersonal Psychology Medical Hypotheses,* and *Gnosis.*

The secrets the mushrooms revealed to me are enclosed in a big book that they [the mushrooms] showed to me. . . . At one point a duende [elf] came toward me. He asked a strange question, "But what do wish to become, you, Maria Sabina?" I answered him, without thinking, that I wished to become a Saint. Then the spirit smiled and immediately he had in his hands something that was not there before, a big Book with many written pages. "Here," he said, "I am

giving you this book so that you can work better and help
people who need help and know the secrets of the world
where everything is known." I thumbed through the leaves
of the Book, many and many written pages, and alas I
thought I didn't know how to read. . . . And suddenly I was
reading, and understanding all that was written. . . . It was
as though I had become richer, wiser, in a moment I learned
millions of things, I learned and learned and learned. . . .

MARIA SABINA, FROM ÁLVARO ESTRADA, *MARIA SABINA*
AND HER MAZATEC MUSHROOM VELADA, 1974

SOCIETY PHOTOGRAPHER ALLAN Richardson later said that what he experienced that night in the darkened room of a hut in the mountains of southern Mexico seemed three thousand miles and a thousand years removed from his home in New York City (Richardson 1990, 196). He and his traveling companion, a Wall Street banker named R. Gordon Wasson, had been invited by Mazatec Indians to participate in a secret religious ceremony that included the ingestion of entheogenic mushrooms. Wasson and Richardson thus became the first white "outsiders" in recorded history to partake of the sacred mushrooms in a Mazatec mushroom *velada* (night vigil). As Wasson described the experience two years later in *Life* magazine:

On the night of June 29–30, 1955, in a Mexican Indian village so remote from the world that most of the people speak no Spanish, my friend Allan Richardson and I shared with a family of Indian friends a celebration of "holy communion" where "divine" mushrooms were first adored and then consumed. The Indians mingled Christian and pre-Christian elements in their religious practices in a way disconcerting for Christians but natural for them. The rite was led by two women, mother and daughter, both of them *curanderas*, or shamans. . . . The mushrooms were of a species with hallucinogenic powers; that is, they cause the eater to see visions. We chewed and swallowed these acrid mushrooms, saw visions, and emerged from the experience awestruck. We had come from afar to attend a mushroom rite but had expected nothing so staggering as the virtuosity of the performing curanderas and the astonishing effects of the mushrooms. (Wasson 1957)

"For the first time," Wasson added, "the word ecstasy took on real meaning. For the first time it did not mean someone else's state of mind" (Wasson 1957). In other words, for the first time, at age fifty-six, he had experienced *enthusiasm* during a religious rite. Ecstatic transports of this type are not uncommon in shamanic rites that utilize entheogens, vigorous dancing, or other techniques to induce altered states of consciousness. But they are rare in mainstream Christian churches, of which modern Pentecostals are the only ones whose worship aims specifically to stimulate a form of religious enthusiasm bearing some resemblance to ecstatic transport. As a lifelong Episcopalian, Wasson had no analogues in his experience with which to compare the religious awe that shook him to the center of his bones that night. Yet his written accounts of the velada represent it in a way that begs comparison, I think, to certain elements of Pentecostal worship.

In the following pages I briefly describe: the known history of the velada, from its suppression by Spanish conquistadors to its relatively recent rediscovery by Westerners, how Wasson and his wife became interested in it and arranged for him and Richardson to be the first outsiders to fully participate, Wasson's written accounts of what they experienced in the velada held on June 29–30, 1955, and a survey of the Pentecostal references found in these accounts. Finally, in my conclusion, I discuss the possibility that Wasson perceived the velada as a prototype for using entheogens as sacramental substances in mainstream Christian worship.

HISTORY OF THE VELADA

The Mazatec mushroom velada represents a syncretic conflation of different religious beliefs that collided and fused at the time of the

Spanish Conquest. Catholic friars who accompanied the Spaniards in the early 1500s found the Indians ingesting mushrooms that reportedly caused visions. The Indians, who called these mushrooms *teonanácatl,* an Aztec word often translated as "god's flesh" or "divine flesh," used them in religious rites of prehistoric provenance. The friars condemned this practice. An example quoted by Wasson is the following sixteenth-century account by Fray Toribio de Benavente called Motolinía:

> They had another way of drunkenness that made them more cruel and it was with some fungi or small mushrooms, which exist in this land as in Castilla; but those of this land are of such a kind that, eaten raw and being bitter, they drink after them or eat them with a little bees' honey; and a while later they would see a thousand visions, especially serpents, and as they would be out of their senses, it would seem to them that their legs and bodies were full of worms eating them alive, and thus half rabid they would sally forth from the house, wanting someone to kill them; and with this bestial drunkenness and travail that they were feeling, it happened sometimes that they hanged themselves, and also against others they were crueler. These mushrooms they called in their language *teunanacatlth* [var. *teonanácatl*], which means "flesh of god," or the devil whom they worshipped; and in this wise with that bitter victual by their cruel god were they houseled. (Wasson 1980, xvii)

According to Wasson, the friars condemned the ritual ingestion of entheogenic mushrooms by the Mazatecs and other Nahua tribes because, in his opinion, they considered this practice to be "an appalling simulacrum of Holy Communion" (Wasson 1980, xviii).

One can imagine the many trembling confabulations of the friars as they would whisper together how to meet this Satanic enemy. The *teonanácatl* struck at the heart of the Christian religion. I need hardly remind my readers of the parallel, the designation of the Elements in our Eucharist: "Take, eat, this is my Body . . . ," and again, "Grant us therefore, gracious Lord, so to eat the flesh of thy dear Son . . . and to drink His blood. . . ." But the truth was even worse. The orthodox Christian must accept on faith the miracle of the conversion of the bread and wine into God's flesh and blood: that is what is meant by the Doctrine of Transubstantiation. By contrast the sacred mushroom of the Aztecs carries its own conviction: every communicant will testify to the miracle that he has experienced. (Wasson 1980, xviii)

Not surprisingly, therefore, the Spaniards made an effort to suppress the mushroom velada and believed that they succeeded. So completely did the practice disappear from the light of day that over time Western scholars concluded that the friars had made a mistake: that teonanácatl was peyote cactus buttons, not mushrooms. However, for hundreds of years, secret mushroom veladas thrived in mountain villages of central and southern Mexico. And while they continued in secret, something interesting happened. Christian concepts began to get mixed with the pagan ones. The mushrooms themselves got conflated with Christ—the story that the mushrooms sprang up from the ground where Christ's blood fell at the time of his Passion is an example (Wasson 1980, 46). Since the mushroom veladas were secret this conflation was not done to please the authorities. Rather, it was spontaneous and sincere—a classic syncretism, such as marked the original spread of Christianity through pagan Europe.

In 1936, a Mexican ethnobotanist named Blas Pablo Reko rebelled against the prevailing scientific view that teonanácatl was peyote. He began to consult with indigenous peoples in the mountains of Oaxaca in south central Mexico about the possible existence of entheogenic mushrooms. They not only confirmed for him their existence, but also revealed that the mushrooms still were used in secret veladas. In 1938 Reko was joined in his field research by a young ethnobotany student from Harvard named Richard Evans Schultes, who secured and identified voucher samples of entheogenic mushrooms in the Mazatec village of Huautla de Jiménez. One year later, a Mexico City anthropologist named Jean Bassett Johnson and his wife, Irmgard Weitlaner, became the first outsiders to attend a mushroom velada, though their hosts did not offer them mushrooms; they participated only as observers. Also that year, Schultes published a paper identifying teonanácatl as a specific mushroom (Schultes 1939; Wasson 1990, 252), but the onset of World War II ensured that it was overlooked for several years.

WASSON'S ROAD TO
THE MUSHROOM VELADA

Meanwhile, Gordon Wasson was pursuing his career as an investment banker at the prestigious Wall Street firm of J. P. Morgan & Co., where he rose to the rank of vice president before retiring in the early 1960s. Descended from British ancestors, he had been born on September 22, 1898, in Great Falls, Montana, and grew up in Newark, New Jersey. His father, Edmund, was a somewhat controversial Episcopal priest who wrote a book in 1914 called *Religion and Drink*, which used Bible references to refute prohibitionists. According to Wasson, his father "never tired of pointing out that Christ's first miracle . . . was the conversion of water into wine (not wine into grape juice), and that the last act of his ministry was to invite his apostles to drink wine in remembrance of him" (Riedlinger 1990, 252). Wasson also told a story of the time his father helped him with a grammar school assignment.

> There came a year when my teacher in school asked us to memorize each week a verse of our own selection from the Bible, and then recite it in class. Our father felt contempt for this homeopathic approach to the vast subject of Bible study, and he conspired with me to find the most absurd, the most embarrassing, verses for me to take to class. Imagine my glee! It was known of course that my

father was a clergyman, and the confusion of my teacher was all the more extreme. After she had called on me two weeks running, she thenceforth ignored my presence. (Wasson 1990, 248)

At home Wasson's father took pains to teach him and his brother a deep appreciation for the Bible. Together they carefully read it from cover to cover three times, with Edmund expounding the text.

according to the latest interpretations of scholars and critics—the Higher Criticism, as this body of Bible exegesis was called. How extraordinary must have been the spectacle of us little boys, in short trousers, prattling about the Vulgate, the Septuagint, the Pentateuch and Hexateuch, the use of Yahweh and Elohim, and of Adonai, interpolations of Priestly Redactors, the reconstructed Sayings of Jesus, and all the other terms then current in Bible study! Moreover, we each learned a verse of the Bible by heart every day, and it was our practice to repeat the nine verses learned on the nine previous days as well. (Wasson 1990, 246)

Thus Wasson was thoroughly versed in the Bible. He retained this knowledge all his life, affirming in his sixties that the Bible "stands in a class by itself, head and shoulders above" even Homer and Herodotus (Wasson 1990, 247). In his opinion,

It is the autobiography of a gifted people, an autobiography in which every facet of the peoples' inner life is exposed eloquently to view, every weakness shown with naked candour, its manner of living and dying, its beliefs as to its own past, its history, its tabus and rules governing the *minutiae* of its daily existence, its aspirations, a wealth of illuminating episodes both fictional and veridical, the poetry and romance of its supreme moments, all expressed in words of matchless splendour. In many intelligent and cultivated circles the Bible suffers today from the people who keep it company, from the proprietary claims on it of extreme sectarians with whom no civilized person cares to consort. (Wasson 1990, 247)

After serving in the army during World War I, Wasson earned his degree in English at Columbia University. Upon graduation he visited London, where he met Valentina (Tina) Pavlovna Guercken, a Russian emigré who was studying to be a pediatrician. He then returned to New York and taught English at Columbia for a year, in 1921,* before taking a job as a business journalist for newspapers in New England. In 1928 he was hired as a banker with the Guaranty Co. of New York and in 1934 joined the staff at J. P. Morgan & Co., where he remained until his retirement in 1963.

Wasson and Tina married in 1926. Their honeymoon, delayed until late summer 1927, was spent in a cabin in the Catskill Mountains. It was there that the mushroom quest started. When out for a walk one day, Tina rushed off the path into the woods to gather mushrooms she saw growing in the shadows. Wasson begged her to stop, fearing Tina was going to poison herself. She just laughed at him and said she would cook them up, which she did upon returning to their cabin. "That evening she ate them, alone," recalled Wasson. "I thought to wake up the next morning a widower" (Wasson 1957). Later he wrote:

This episode made so deep an impression on us that from then on, as circumstances permitted, we gathered all the information that we could about the attitude of various peoples toward mushrooms—what kinds they know, their names for them, the etymology of those names, the folklore and legends in which mushrooms figure, references to them in proverbs and literature and mythology. (Wasson 1959)

---

*One of Wasson's students who remembered him was poet Langston Hughes: "As for the instructors at Columbia whom I knew, the only one who interested me much was a Mr. Wasson, who read Mencken aloud all the time." Hughes, L. *The Big Sea*. New York: Thunder Mouth Press, 1986: 84.

By the 1940s and early '50s they were working together on a Russian cookbook, *Mushrooms, Russia and History: An Introduction to Russia through the Kitchen*. One long chapter on mushrooms grew bigger and bigger, until it became the whole book. Based on their research the two of them wondered if mushrooms may not have been worshipped or used sacramentally by ancient Europeans. Thus some Europeans—the Russians and Czechs, for example—now regard them with delight, while others, such as the English, regard them with suspicion, even horror. Wasson and Tina theorized that both intense reactions are degraded forms of what had once been powerful religious awe.

Tina happened to mention this theory to their friend Robert Graves, who told them in the early 1950s of Schultes's paper on teonanácatl, which he had seen footnoted in a newsletter published by a pharmaceutical company. Wasson and Tina promptly contacted Schultes, who by then had assumed the position of director of Harvard Botanical Museum, and Schultes referred them to his contacts in the village of Huautla de Jiménez.

Thus it was that, beginning in 1953, Wasson, sometimes accompanied by Tina and their teenage daughter Mary (Masha), made the first of ten annual visits to the Oaxaca region. In 1953 they sat in on a mushroom velada but were not invited to participate. The male shaman who presided said the mushrooms had the power to take those who ingested them *"ahí donde Dios está"*—there where God is (Wasson and Wasson 1957, 294). Wasson noted at this time that the mushrooms are treated respectfully by the Indians, so he always made it a point to do likewise. "After all," he wrote, "it was a bold thing we were doing, strangers probing the innermost secrets of this remote people. How would a Christian priest receive a pagan's request for samples of the Host" (Wasson and Wasson 1957, 250)?

THE VELADA OF JUNE 29–30, 1955

Beginning in 1954 Wasson hired Allan Richardson to accompany him on the next few expeditions and take photographs. These were difficult journeys by foot and by mule on deplorable mountain roads winding over the mountains to villages such as Mazatlán and Huautla at elevations up to a mile and a half. At first they succeeded only in compiling information about the velada—for example, that it is not a regularly scheduled event such as Christian worship services but rather is convened for "healing" purposes, broadly defined. Therefore the shaman who conducts it holds the title *curandera* if a woman, *curandero* if a man; both words mean "healer." Furthermore, mushroom veladas are not strictly liturgical though they are ritualized with the mushroom used sacramentally.

A breakthrough came on June 29, 1955, when Wasson and Richardson met Cayetano and Guadelupe García, a married couple living at the edge of town in Huautla. That afternoon, the Garcías and some of their friends took Wasson and Richardson down the mountainside to gather entheogenic mushrooms growing on sugar cane refuse. The mushroom they gathered, *Psilocybe caerulescens,* is locally known as the "landslide mushroom," either because of the cascading visions it evokes or because of the way that it grows, in clustered masses resembling an avalanche.

Cayetano then sent his brother, an interpreter, along with Wasson and Richardson to meet a shaman who lived in Huautla by the name of María Sabina. Believing that she had no choice because Wasson had apparently been authorized by Cayetano, an official of the town, she agreed to conduct a velada that evening with her daughter Apollonia at the home of the Garcías. María was then about fifty-five years old, the same age as Wasson. Guadelupe described her to him as *"una Señora sin mancha,* a lady without blemish, immaculate, one who had never dishonored her calling by using her personal powers for evil" (Wasson and Wasson 1957, 289). To Wasson she seemed "the hierophant, the thaumaturge, the psychopompos, in whom the troubles and aspirations of countless generations of mankind had found, were still finding, their relief" (Wasson 1980, 28). He later recalled:

On that last Wednesday of June, after nightfall, we gathered [at about 8:15] in the lower chamber. . . . In all, at one time or another, there must have been twenty-five persons present. . . . Both Allan . . . [and I] were deeply impressed by the mood of the gathering. We were received and the night's events unrolled in an atmosphere of simple friendliness that reminded us of the agape of early Christian times. . . . We were mindful of the drama of the situation. We were attending as participants a mushroomic Supper of unique anthropological interest, which was being held pursuant to a tradition of unfathomed age, possibly going back to the time when the remote ancestors of our hosts were living in Asia, back perhaps to the dawn of man's cultural history, when he was discovering the idea of God. (Wasson and Wasson 1957, 289)

The ceremony started at about 10:30 when María and her daughter took their positions before a small table that served as their altar. Photos were not allowed in this first session once the mushrooms took effect, leaving Richardson nothing to do but ride out the experience. Apparently no photos have survived that show Wasson consuming his mushrooms, though he took one of Richardson eating his share, which accompanied the article in *Life*. In this photo Richardson appears somewhat worried, perhaps because he was remembering the promise he made to his wife not to let "those nasty toadstools" touch his lips (Wasson 1957). He did so anyway because, he later explained, he did not want to risk insulting his Indian hosts.

Wasson noted during this and later veladas he attended that the Mazatecs normally follow a certain procedure with ritual overtones. The healer first praises the mushrooms while passing them through the smoke of copal incense to purify them before handing them out to the other participants. Wasson and Richardson each ate about six pairs of mushrooms, which in a velada are always distributed in pairs and eaten facing the altar. María's dose was twice as much. After the mushrooms are eaten, all the candles are extinguished (veladas always take place after dark), followed by silence for about twenty minutes. The healer then starts humming, and the humming eventually modulates into a chant that continues at intervals throughout the night. María's songs put Wasson in mind of "age-old chants" that sometimes seemed to him "soaked in weary melancholy" (Wasson 1980, 19). They were punctuated by percussive sound effects produced when María and her daughter clapped their hands and thumped their chests. Much of the chanting involved a declaration by María of her spiritual credentials, such as this from a later velada:

> *Woman of space am I,*
> *Woman of day am I,*
> *Woman of light am I, . . .*
> *Lawyer woman am I, woman of affairs am I,*
> *I give account to the judge,*
> *And I give account to the government,*
> *And I give account to the Father Jesus Christ,*
> *And mother princess, my patron mother, oh Jesus, Father*
>   *Jesus Christ,*
> *Woman of danger am I, woman of beauty am I, . . .*
> *I am going to the sky [heaven], Jesus Christ, . . .*
> *Whirling woman of the whirlwind am I, woman of a*
>   *sacred, enchanted place am I,*
> *Eagle woman am I, and clock woman am I,*
> *Isn't that so now? . . .*
> *With breast milk, with dew,*
> *The world can be cheered up, let's cheer up, let's be*
>   *enlightened.*
> *Let our Father come out to us, let Christ come out to us,*
> *We wait for our Father, we wait for our Father, we wait for*
>   *Christ, with calmness, with care,*
> *Man of breast milk, man of dew,*
> *Fresh man, tender man, . . .*

And there I give account, [the mushroom] says,
There I give account to him face to face, before your glory,
    [the mushroom] says,
There I give him account, [the mushroom] says,
Yes, Jesus Christ says, there I have an owner, [the
    mushroom] says . . . (Halifax 1979, 203–5)

At about 11:20 p.m., Richardson reported feeling chilly just before the visions started. A notebook, now in my possession, that he had brought with him intending to write down his experiences as they occurred contains only a few scribbled entries as the mushrooms took effect. His handwriting quickly becomes almost illegible after the intriguing statement, "Spirit comes down from above." In *Mushrooms, Russia and History*, Wasson tells what happened next in words of great beauty and piety. Speaking for Richardson as well as for himself, he reports that they first saw

geometric patterns, angular not circular, in richest colors, such as might adorn textiles or carpets. Then the patterns grew into architectural structures, with colonnades and architraves, patios of regal splendor, the stone-work all in brilliant colors, gold and onyx and ebony, all most harmoniously and ingeniously contrived, in richest magnificence extending beyond the reach of sight, in vistas measureless to man. . . . They seemed to belong . . . to the imaginary architecture described by the visionaries of the Bible. (Wasson and Wasson 1957, 293)

This was obviously something very different from the horrible visions ascribed to the mushrooms by Fray Toribio de Benavente, who presumably did not try them before writing about them. In Wasson's case (and Richardson's), the experience was more like an epiphany:

There is no better way to describe the sensation than to say it was as though . . . [my] very soul had been scooped out of . . . [my] body and translated to a point floating in space, leaving behind the husk of clay . . . [my] body . . . We had the sensation that the walls of our humble house had vanished, that our untrammeled souls were floating in the universe, stroked by divine breezes, possessed of a divine mobility that would transport us anywhere on the wings of a thought. . . . There came a moment when it seemed as though the visions themselves were about to be transcended, and dark gates reaching upward beyond sight were about to part, and we were to find ourselves in the presence of the Ultimate. We seemed to be flying at the dark gates as a swallow at a dazzling lighthouse, and the gates were to part and admit us. But they did not open, and with a thud we fell back, gasping. We felt disappointed, but also frightened and half relieved, that we had not entered into the presence of the Ineffable, whence, it seemed to us at the time, we might not have returned, for we had sensed that a willing extinction in the divine radiance had been awaiting us. (Wasson and Wasson 1957, 293–95)

After the visions had diminished in intensity, Wasson and Richardson fell asleep at about 4:00 a.m., waking two hours later to enjoy some bread and chocolate with their hosts. When Wasson later asked Cayetano what he could pay him for having arranged the velada, the Indian "turned to his wife and let her speak. *'No hicimos esto por dinero,'* she said, which is to say, 'We did not do this for money,' and they would accept none" (Wasson and Wasson 1957, 304). Two days later Wasson ate mushrooms again in another velada conducted by María in the same house. Richardson was present but did not participate. Having decided that once was enough, he never again took the mushrooms (Richardson 1990, 198). Wasson, however, went on to ingest them about thirty times (Riedlinger 1990, 215), both in Mazatec Indian rituals and at home.

In the years before his death due to stroke or heart failure on

December 23, 1986, he published numerous scholarly books in addition to *Mushrooms, Russia and History* on the subject of the use of sacred mushrooms in various cultures. He was cremated and his ashes interred in a closed columbarium adjacent to the Chapel of St. Joseph of Arimathea in the Washington Cathedral.

The Mazatecs, meanwhile, came under pressure from several quarters soon after Wasson published his *Life* magazine article, even though he used false names for María (Eva Mendez), her fellow Indians, and the town of Huautla. In any case, pseudonyms would not have fooled the local Christian missionaries. Two of them, Eunice Pike and Florence Cowan, published a paper with the ominous title "Mushroom Ritual vs. Christianity" in a 1959 issue of the Christian journal *Practical Anthropology*. In it they wonder, "How can one effectively present the message of divine revelation to a people who already have, according to their belief, a means whereby anyone who so desires may get messages directly from the supernatural world via a more spectacular and immediately satisfying way than Christianity has to offer" (Pike and Cowan 1959)? The authors then answer their own question:

> The thing that has helped is study of the Scriptures . . . until the person concerned comes to understand God's idea of sin, his love and plan for the sinner, and something of God's greatness. That seldom happens after the study of a few brief passages; it seems to take a considerable amount before a person's eyes are opened. (Pike and Cowan 1959)

More immediately damaging was the attention that Wasson's *Life* article brought from a variety of seekers who flocked to Huautla in search of enlightenment or simply a good high. Included among them were hippies, beatniks, rock stars, and journalists whose sometimes inappropriate behavior made life difficult for people in Huautla. Things got worse when *federales,* under pressure from the Mexican and U.S. governments, threatened to prosecute anyone using the mushrooms, on the grounds that they were trafficking in dangerous drugs. At one point angry townspeople burned down María's house because they blamed her for having made public their long-standing secret, but eventually they reconciled with her. By the time she died in 1985, at age eighty-seven, she was regarded with honor not only in Huautla but also throughout Mexico. It later was reported that

> Father Antonio Reyes Hernandez, the Catholic Bishop who resides in the parish where María Sabina lived, never admonished or condemned her for her work in the village. He was aware that her rituals and practices had been handed down to her through the ages from her ancestors. He knew that her services were valid treatments for those who sought her shamanic talents. Father Hernandez also recognized that her work with the sick and suffering was the mark of a true Christian—one willing to help the less fortunate. Although he knew that Doña María used the mushroom and pagan practice to heal and cure, he also understood that María Sabina's nature was not of a demonic spirit, satanic or even heretic. He appreciated her spirituality and treasured her work as a life-long member of his church. . . . As Doña María believed in the power of Christ, she also believed in the power of the mushrooms. (Allen 1994)

PENTECOSTAL ELEMENTS IN THE MUSHROOM VELADA

The Pentecostal elements that seem to be part of Wasson's written accounts of the mushroom velada do not necessarily indicate that he was familiar with Pentecostalism. Rather, these writings are keyed to certain sections of the Bible that inspired the beginning of the modern Pentecostal movement, especially chapters 1 and 2 of Acts of the Apostles. There it is reported that Jesus "presented himself alive" to his disciples several days after his crucifixion and stayed with them for forty days. During that time, Jesus instructed his disciples to wait in Jerusalem for a sign—a baptism by the Holy Spirit that would imbue them with power. When he left them again, reportedly ascending into heaven, his apostles took up residence in "the room upstairs" (or "upper chamber") of a building in Jerusalem, where they and "certain women, including Mary the mother of Jesus," constantly devoted themselves to prayer. What transpired, circa 34 C.E., is described as follows in Acts 2:1–17:*

> When the day of Pentecost had come, they were all together in one place. And suddenly from heaven there came a sound like the rush of a violent wind, and it filled the entire house where they were sitting. Divided tongues, as of fire, appeared among them, and a tongue rested on each of them. All of them were filled with the Holy Spirit and began to speak in other languages, as the Spirit gave them ability. Now there were devout Jews from every nation under heaven living in Jerusalem. And at this sound the crowd gathered and was bewildered because each one heard them speaking in the native language of each. Amazed and astonished, they asked, "Are not all these who are speaking Galileans [i.e., followers of Jesus the Galilean]? And how is it that we hear, each of us, in our own native language?" . . . All were amazed and perplexed, saying to one another, "What does this mean?" But others sneered and said, "They are filled with new wine." But Peter, standing with the eleven [apostles], raised his voice and addressed them, "Men of Judea and all who live in Jerusalem, let this be known to you, and listen to what I say. Indeed, these are not drunk, as you suppose, for it is only nine o'clock in the morning. No, this is what was spoken through the prophet Joel [in Joel 2:28–32]:

---

*All biblical quotations are from: *The Harper Collins Study Bible, New Revised Standard Version.* New York: HarperCollins, 1989.

'In the last days it will be,
God declares,
that I will pour out my Spirit
upon all flesh,
and your sons and your
daughters shall prophesy,
and your young men shall
see visions,
and your old men shall
dream dreams. . . .' "

William Joseph Seymour, who founded the modern Pentecostal movement in Los Angeles in 1906, believed that the Christian church had lost its way soon after this first Christian Pentecost by getting too dogmatic and that consequently few of the wonders foretold had come to pass. To rectify this he preached an alternative form of worship that encourages "speaking in tongues" (glossolalia), trances, faith healing, visions, dreams, and other such manifestations of enthusiasm. Pentecostals believe that these states are induced when a person is filled with the Holy Spirit, usually during a worship service. Most of them also believe that the end times are near, when the kingdom of God will prevail. In the meantime, they experience brief previews of this kingdom when the Spirit enters into them during their practice of what Harvard theologian Harvey Cox has labeled "primal spirituality" (Cox 1995, 17).

The emphasis here is on "practice." Cox points out that "while the beliefs of the fundamentalists, and of many other religious groups, are enshrined in formal theological systems, those of Pentecostalism are imbedded in testimonies, ecstatic speech, and bodily movement" (Cox 1995, 15). Thus their meetings, which initially were held whenever possible in upper rooms to simulate the setting of the Pentecost described in Acts of the Apostles (Anderson 1992, 77), are liturgically designed to encourage such outbursts of "glory" (Anderson 1992, 69), which believers ascribe to a kind of possession by the Holy Spirit. For while Pentecostal worship does include the historical practice of baptizing people in water, Pentecostals interpret Acts 1:5 as a mandate for Christians to also seek a second "Spirit baptism." Many interpret Joel's prophecy quoted by Peter to mean that the end times will involve a "latter rain" of Spirit pouring down, empowering people to prophesy and have visions in addition to other miraculous signs such as faith healing.

The Mazatec mushroom velada likewise has no formal theology, calls down an empowering Spirit as its pivotal event, includes healing, and accommodates enthusiastic outbursts in the form of spontaneous utterances, walking toward the altar on one's knees, prolonged ecstatic dancing, and similarly pious demonstrations (Wasson and Wasson 1957, 296–98). Its participants, like those who attended the first Christian Pentecost, include both women and men; in fact, the velada may be led by either gender. And Wasson's pointed observation that the velada of June 29–30, 1955 took place in a "lower chamber" seems to echo, in reversal, the New Testament report that the first Christian Pentecost occurred in an "upper chamber." Before discussing the significance of these and other similarities between Pentecostal and Mazatec Christianity it needs to be recalled that Wasson's training in the Bible was exceptionally rigorous. It is therefore unlikely that any apparent allusion to biblical concepts in his writing is an accident. For example, the chapter in *Mushrooms, Russia and History* containing Wasson's first detailed account of the mushroom velada of June 29–30, 1955, is titled "Teonanácatl" and subtitled "The Mushroom Agape." We have already heard that he compared this "agape" to that of "early Christian times" (Wasson and Wasson 1957, 289). The prototypical Christian agape is, of course, the Pentecostal gathering described in chapter 2 of Acts of the Apostles. We have also heard that sixteenth-century friars denounced the state of mind evoked by mushrooms as mere drunkenness, a charge that Wasson refutes on behalf of his Indian hosts when he observes, "The proceedings went forward with an easy decorum. Neither on this occasion nor at any other time or place did we see or hear the mushrooms treated as a subject for jocularity, of the kind that marks the use of alcohol among fully civilized peoples" (Wasson and Wasson 1957, 289–90). Peter likewise defended his fellow Christians when outsiders confused their enthusiasm with inebriation.

According to Wasson, two "holy pictures" were displayed on the table that served as an altar for the velada (Wasson and Wasson 1957, 291). One depicted Jesus as a child, the other, his baptism in the Jordan River. This confirmed that the Indians viewed their mushroom service as related in some basic way to Christianity. Furthermore, Wasson reports, "The Señora had asked us to take care not to invade the corner of the room on the left of the altar table, for down that corner would descend the Holy Ghost" (Wasson and Wasson 1957, 292). Later, as the mushrooms took effect, she reportedly talked "as though invoking the Spirits or as though the Holy Ghost was speaking through the mushrooms. We heard the names of Christ (which she pronounced with an intrusive 'r,' *Khristos*), of St. Peter and St. Paul" (Wasson and Wasson 1957, 297). These spoken utterances differed from the chanting, Wasson said, in being "fresh and vibrant and rich in expressiveness. The mushrooms were talking to the point" (Wasson and Wasson 1957, 297). By this he meant that her pronouncements sounded more authoritative than her chanting, which outsiders such as Wasson, who did not speak the Mazatec language, tend to experience as rambling and monotonous.

Moreover, Wasson almost certainly perceived the ecstasis evoked by the mushrooms as something akin to possession by the Christian Holy Spirit, relative to which María's chanting was perhaps a ritual beckoning. That is how I interpret the emphasis he placed on the following anecdote. During one of his first visits to Oaxaca he was told by Eunice Pike, the Christian missionary, that the Mazatec language term for the mushrooms translates to "the dear little tykes that leap forth" (Wasson 1980, 45). A Spanish-speaking Indian later explained to him that

El honguillo viene por sí mismo, no se sabe de dónde, como el viento que viene sin saber de dónde ni porqué.

The little mushroom comes of itself, no one knows whence, like the wind that comes we know not whence nor why. (Wasson 1980, 45)

Wasson clearly saw something significant in this explanation, first because he quotes it as a couplet and second because he so often repeats it in his many books and papers. In light of his rigorous Bible training, it seems likely that he must have remembered the following words of Jesus in John 3:5–8:

Very truly, I tell you, no one can enter the kingdom of God without being born of water and Spirit. What is born of the flesh is flesh, and what is born of the Spirit is spirit. Do not be astonished when I say to you, "You must be born from above." *The wind blows where it chooses, and you hear the sound of it, but you do not know where it comes from or where it goes.* So it is with everyone who is born of the Spirit. [emphasis added]

This biblical connection—reinforced, as we shall see, by other comments made by Wasson in his writings—introduces an important concept. He seems to be suggesting that the Mazatecs regard the capricious emergence of their teonanácatl from the earth as a form of gratuitous grace bestowed by God's Spirit. Like Jesus when he was alive, the mushroom both embodies and proclaims this Spirit. As such it comprises an *actual* grace, which enables those who eat it to experience God's presence. In effect they are transported to God's "kingdom," much as Pentecostal worshippers believe that when the Spirit enters into them they preview in the "already" what will come in the "not yet" at the end of historical time. I think that Wasson is describing something similar when he relates that the mushrooms "took full and sweeping possession" of him (Wasson and Wasson 1957, 295), temporarily transporting him "there where God is" (Wasson and Wasson 1957, 294). Recall that his visions reminded him of those that are reported in the Bible, such as "resplendent palaces all laid over with semiprecious stones," "mountains rising tier above tier to the very heavens," "gardens of ineffable beauty," and "river estuaries, pellucid waters flowing through an endless expanse of reeds down to a measureless sea, all by the pastel light of a horizontal sun" (Wasson 1957; Wasson and Wasson 1957, 294–95). These descriptions clearly echo certain features of biblical Eden, the garden of God, which according to Genesis 2:8–14 was watered by a river with four estuaries running through a land containing gold and onyx—precious substances also found, along with "stones of fire" (apparently meaning gems), at the site of God's holy mountain in the Eden of Ezekiel 28:11–14. Of the objects he saw in his visions, Wasson says:

> No patina of age hung on them. They were all fresh from God's workshop, pristine in their finish. . . . They seemed the very archetypes of beautiful form and color. We felt ourselves in the presence of the Ideas that Plato had talked about. In saying this let not the reader think that we are indulging in rhetoric, straining to command his attention by an extravagant figure of speech. For the world our visions were and must remain "hallucinations." But for us they were not false or shadowy suggestions of real things, figments of an unhinged imagination. What we were seeing was, we knew, the only reality, of which the counterparts of every day are mere imperfect adumbrations. (Wasson and Wasson 1957, 294)

Thus it is that the mushrooms, according to Wasson, "express religion in its purest essence, without intellectual content" (Wasson, Ruck, and Hofmann 1978, 23). They stimulate a mystical experience that cannot be reduced to words or concepts, much in contrast to most Christian worship based on "learned" theological systems. In that sense the Christian religion of the Mazatec mushroom eaters is defined, like Pentecostalism, not by doctrine or by dogma but phenomenologically. Both religions are examples of the primal spirituality that Cox describes as "reaching beyond the levels of creed and ceremony into the core of human religiousness, into . . . that largely unprocessed nucleus of the psyche in which the unending struggle for a sense of purpose and significance goes on" (Cox 1995, 81). Although necessarily subjective, such experiences foster the formation of communities as other people validate this purpose and significance according to shared or consensual beliefs, as Wasson learned firsthand from his Indian hosts. Surrounded in the darkness by an "irregular chorus, subdued in volume, of ecstatic exclamations from the Indians reclining on the ground" (Wasson and Wasson 1957, 299), he experienced something with them that was remarkably like an event at the original Christian Pentecost.

> Confined though we were in a room without windows or open door, at one point we felt a swish of air, just as if we were really suspended in the great outdoors. Was this too an hallucination? If so, all shared it, for when the wind blew on us, there was a general excitement, flashlights were switched on, and our Indian friends were sitting up, amazed at being stroked by the Divine Afflatus. (Wasson and Wasson 1957, 299)

This strengthens the linkage already suggested between the Holy Spirit and the Mazatec Indian concept that the mushrooms come "no one knows whence, like the wind that comes we know not whence nor why." It also strengthened the sense of community that Wasson and Richardson shared with their Indian hosts. For when they lit what Wasson calls, a few lines later, their "electric torches" (Wasson and Wasson 1957, 300), euphemistically suggesting tongues of flame, he saw María

> in a state of excitement, her eyes flashing, her smile no longer that grave smile which we had observed before, but now quick with animation and, if we may use the word, *caritas*. For there is another aspect to the mushrooms that we must mention. The spirit of the agape of which we have already spoken was a prelude to a wave of generous or tender feelings that the mushroom aroused in everyone. . . . On the two nights that we passed in Cayetano's house, we were

aware of no erotic stimulation among those present and we think there was none. But the feeling of brotherly love was strong indeed. Twice in the course of that first night the Señora reached out her right hand to [me] and sought contact with [my] fingers in friendly greeting, across the chasm of the language barrier. The Indians of Middle America are known for their reticence in the display of affection, even within the family circle. It was now clear that the mushrooms emancipate them from inhibitions of this kind. (Wasson and Wasson 1957, 300)

In sum, concluded Wasson, the mushrooms "transport one for the nonce to heaven, where all the senses unite in a joyous symphony shot through with an overwhelming feeling of caritas, of peace and affection for the fellow communicants" (Wasson 1980, xvii). The effect is a transcendence of the barriers existing between people, including—as Wasson observed, no doubt remembering the Pentecostal miracle in Acts—the chasm of the language barrier.

CONCLUSIONS

We have heard that the Mazatec Indians and Wasson both interpreted the mystical ecstasis evoked by the mushrooms as somehow connected with God, Jesus Christ, and the Holy Spirit. Furthermore, Wasson's description of the velada seems to correspond significantly with much of the New Testament account of the original Christian Pentecost. An additional twist is the following observation made by Wasson in his 1980 book *The Wondrous Mushroom*. Recalling that María had informed him that "the Word" (which he had previously called the Holy Ghost) would come down to the left of the altar, he noted that she had explained to Álvaro Estrada in a book about her life.

. . . *veo que el Lenguaje cae, viene de arriba, como si fuesen peque-ños objetos luminosos que caen del cielo. El Lenguaje cae sobre le mesa*

*sagrada, cae sobre mi cuerpo. Entonces atrapo con mis manos palabra
por palabra.*

. . . I see the Word fall, come down from above, as though they were
little luminous objects falling from heaven. The Word falls on the
Holy Table, on my body: with my hand I catch them, Word for
Word. (Wasson 1980, 13)

Compare Wasson's translation to that of Henry Munn in the
English edition of Estrada's book, which came out one year later. There
María is quoted as saying: ". . . I also see that words fall, they come from
up above, as if they were little luminous objects falling from the sky.
The Language falls on the sacred table, falls on my body. Then with
my hands I catch word after word" (Estrada 1981, 94). Was it the Word
that fell, or words? While Munn's translation is perhaps more literally
accurate, Wasson's is presumably more faithful to María's point of view,
insofar as he was present and alert to every nuance of her performance.
In that case, her description calls to mind the "latter rain" prophecy
that Spirit will someday pour down upon the flesh, producing prophe-
cies, visions, and dreams. It could even be argued that Wasson's *Life*
article fulfilled or helped prepare for the fulfillment of this prophecy by
introducing entheogenic mushrooms to the Western world. Certainly,
it was a factor in launching the so-called psychedelic movement of the
early 1960s—even Timothy Leary's first "trip" was on mushrooms
in Mexico (Leary 1995, 11–34)—which resulted in an estimated ten
million people using entheogens by 1977 in the United States alone
(Grinspoon and Bakalar 1979, 79). Alexander Shulgin, who once shared
a room with Wasson for a week at an Esalen conference where both
were featured speakers, came away with the opinion that

he thought his most lasting contribution was allowing that article
in *Life* to appear, and to appear in the form that it took. It was, for
many devout and curious readers of the magazine, their first exposure to the concept of a union between nature and God. And that

there are many different ways to be in the presence of God. And that a lowly mushroom, like ordinary bread and wine, can allow, can insist that you identify with and acknowledge the divine. (Shulgin 1990, 228)

What then shall we make of Wasson's statements, which also appear in *The Wondrous Mushroom,* that today we cannot accept that entheogens speak "with the voice of God" and that "the awe and reverence that these plants once evoked" in traditional cultures such as that of the Mazatecs are "gone for good" (Wasson 1980, xxiii)? I believe that he meant this ironically—that such statements are perhaps a thinly veiled provocation. Wasson once made a similar comment to me when I visited him in his home near the end of his life, in 1985. We had been talking about U.S. government prohibitions that ban the possession and use of the mushroom and other entheogens. Wasson said that he thought they would nonetheless return to popularity in ten to thirty years. His explanation for the temporary setback was that "people don't want to be awed these days" (Riedlinger 1990, 214). He certainly did not impress me as believing that the spiritual potential of the mushroom and other entheogens is gone for good. In fact, he elsewhere states without qualification that the "advantage of the mushroom is that it puts many, if not everyone, within reach" of having mystical experiences. "It permits you to see, more clearly than our perishing mortal eye can see, vistas beyond the horizons of this life, to travel backwards and forwards in time, to enter other planes of existence, even (as the Indians say) to know God" (Wasson, Ruck, and Hofmann 1978, 19). His opinion of what this portends for Christian worship is likewise unequivocal.

. . . God's flesh! How those words echo down the centuries of religious experience! (In the Book of Common Prayer, in the Prayer of Humble Access, the faithful are summoned to eat "the flesh of thy dear son Jesus Christ.") The Christian doctrine of Transubstantiation is a hard saying, calling for great faith. . . . The Mexican Indian with his teonanácatl has no need for Transubstantiation because his mushroom speaks for itself. By comparison with the mushroom, the Element in the [formalized, post-Pentecostal] Christian agape seems pallid. The mushroom holds the key to a mystical union with God, whereas only rare souls can attain similar ecstasy and divine communion by intensive contemplation of the miracle of the Mass. (Wasson and Wasson 1957, 319)

That Wasson regarded the mushrooms to be an authentic such key was abundantly clear to María Sabina. She stated that he and his friends were the first to come seeking the mushrooms not "because they suffered from any illness. Their reason was that they came to find God. Before Wasson nobody took the mushrooms only to find God" (Estrada 1981, 73). What he and Richardson experienced was therefore not the same as it was and had been for their Indian hosts, and what they took away with them had different implications for the Western world. In that sense it is true, as Wasson noted, that the "Old Order does not mix with the New. The wisdom of the *Sabia* [Wise Ones], genuine though it was, has nothing to give to the world of tomorrow" (Wasson 1980, 223). In other words, it cannot be appropriated whole; it cannot be transplanted from one culture to another and retain its indigenous purity. As Paul advised the early Christians, there are many different voices in the world that are meaningful unto themselves, but if I do not understand them, "I will be a foreigner to the speaker and the speaker a foreigner to me" (1 Corinthians 14:10–11). Often it is possible, however, for different cultures to assimilate "translations" of each other's wisdom. When this occurs they do not mix in the sense that an Old Order might be subsumed to a New one or vice versa. Rather, both evolve into something entirely different, a syncretic transformation.

Wasson knew that the velada he attended on the evening of June 29–30, 1955, was quite different from what it must have been before the conquest. He knew that many centuries ago the Mazatec Indians combined what was to them a new religion, Christianity, with their ancient pagan practices, producing a syncretic hybrid focused on physical healing. Is it not feasible that modern Christianity could likewise adopt certain elements of this indigenous hybrid, producing an experiential form of Christian worship in the Pentecostal mode that uses entheogens for calling down the Spirit?

REFERENCES

Allen, J. "Chasing the Ghost of María Sabina." *Psychedelic Illuminations* no. 6 (1994).

Anderson, R. M. *Vision of the Disinherited: The Making of American Pentecostalism.* Peabody, Mass.: Hendrickson, 1992.

Cox, H. *Fire from Heaven: The Rise of Pentecostal Spirituality and the Reshaping of Religion in the Twenty-first Century.* Reading, Mass.: Addison-Wesley, 1995.

Estrada, Á. *María Sabina: Her Life and Chants.* Translation and commentary by Henry Munn. Santa Barbara, Calif.: Ross-Erikson, 1981.

Grinspoon, L., and J. B. Bakalar. *Psychedelic Drugs Reconsidered.* New York: Basic Books, 1979.

Halifax, J. *Shamanic Voices: A Survey of Visionary Narratives.* New York: E. P. Dutton, 1979.

Leary, T. *High Priest.* Berkeley, Calif.: Ronin Press, 1995.

Pike, E., and F. Cowan. "Mushroom Ritual vs. Christianity." *Practical Anthropology* 6 (4): (1959) 145–50.

Richardson, A. B. "Recollections of R. Gordon Wasson's 'Friend and Photographer.'" In *The Sacred Mushroom Seeker: Essays for R. Gordon Wasson.* Edited by T. J. Riedlinger. Portland, Ore.: Dioscorides Press, 1990. All unattributed facts in "Sacred Mushroom Pentecost" are based on information from this book.

Riedlinger, T. J., ed. *The Sacred Mushroom Seeker: Essays for R. Gordon Wasson.* Portland, Ore.: Dioscorides Press, 1990.

Schultes, R. E. "The Identification of Teonanacatl, a Narcotic Basidiomycete of the Aztecs." *Botanical Museum Leaflets.* Cambridge, Mass.: Harvard University 7 (3) (1939): 37–54.

Shulgin, A. "Celebrating Gordon Wasson." In *The Sacred Mushroom Seeker: Essays for R. Gordon Wasson.* Edited by T. J. Riedlinger. Portland, Ore.: Dioscorides Press, 1990.

Wasson, R. G. "Seeking the Magic Mushroom." *Life,* May 17, 1957, 100–20.

——. "The Hallucinogenic Mushrooms of Mexico: An Adventure in Ethnomycological Exploration." *Transactions of the New York Academy of Sciences, Series II* 21 (4) (1959): 325–39.

——. *The Wondrous Mushroom: Mycolatry in Mesoamerica.* New York: McGraw-Hill, 1980.

——. "Gordon Wasson's Account of His Childhood." In *The Sacred Mushroom Seeker: Essays for R. Gordon Wasson.* Edited by J. Riedlinger. Portland, Ore.: Dioscorides Press, 1990.

Wasson, R. G., C. A. P. Ruck, and A. Hofmann. *The Road to Eleusis: Unveiling the Secret of the Mysteries.* New York: Harcourt Brace Jovanovich, 1978.

Wasson, V. P., and R. G. Wasson. *Mushrooms, Russia and History.* New York: Pantheon Books, 1957.

10 PSYCHEDELIC EXPERIENCE AND SPIRITUAL PRACTICE

An Interview with Jack Kornfield

Robert Forte

Jack Kornfield trained as a Buddhist monk in the monasteries of Thailand, India, and Burma. A cofounder of the Insight Meditation Society in Barre, Massachusetts, and Spirit Rock in Woodacre, California, he has taught meditation internationally since 1974. Dr. Kornfield holds a Ph.D. in clinical psychology and is a husband and a father. His books include *Living Buddhist Masters, A Path with Heart, Buddha's Little Instruction Book, Teachings of the Buddha, Seeking the Heart of Wisdom* (with Joseph Goldstein), *Living Dharma, A Still Forest Pool,* and *Stories of the Spirit, Stories of the Heart.* www.jackkornfield.com.

> *When sitting in meditation you may have strange experiences or visions such as seeing lights, angels, or buddhas. When you see such things, you should observe yourself first to find out what state the mind is in. Do not forget the basic*

point. Pay attention. Do not wish for visions to arise or not to arise. If you go running after such experiences, you may end up babbling senselessly because the mind has fled the stable. When such things do come, contemplate them. When you have contemplated them, do not be deluded by them. You should consider that they are not yourself; they too are impermanent, unsatisfactory, and not self. Though they have come about, do not take them seriously. . . . Do not take anything as yourself—everything is only a vision or a construction of the mind, a deception that causes you to like, grasp, or fear. When you see such constructions, do not get involved. All unusual experiences and visions are of value to the wise person but harmful to the unwise. Keep practicing until you are not stirred by them.

CHAH, *A STILL FOREST POOL,* 1982

The goal, it cannot be stressed too often, is not religious experiences: it is the religious life. And with respect to the latter, psychedelic "theophanies" can abort a quest as readily as, perhaps more readily than, they further it.

HUSTON SMITH, *FORGOTTEN TRUTH,* 1976

Robert Forte: *Jack, thanks very much for sharing your perspective. With so much said about psychedelic experience and spirituality it may help to look at psychedelics from within an extant spiritual discipline. There is a great deal in Buddhism that can illuminate psychedelic phenomena and help us to understand the curative effect—when there is a curative effect. Maybe a Buddhist perspective can help us to maximize the positive effects of psychedelic experiences and improve or reduce the negative ones.*

Jack Kornfield: There are a couple of things I want to start with, some thoughts I have had on the subject, and we can go on from there.

The first is a statement in answer to your question, which asks for a Buddhist point of view on psychedelics. It is important to say that there is no Buddhist point of view on psychedelics. They are rarely found in the Buddhist tradition, if at all, and generally would be lumped in the precepts under "intoxicants." In the Zen, Vajrayana, and Theravada traditions, the three largest living traditions, there is very little mention of them, very little written, and there is no traditional point of view about the use of them. It is important to understand that. What points of view we have come from our understanding of Buddhist masters and teachers based on contemporary experience. But there is not a traditional body of knowledge in relationship to these substances that I know of.

A second point to make is that, unlike in Hinduism, which at least in its modern form uses a variety of mind-altering substances—particularly things like hashish that some *sadhus* use sitting by the river Ganges smoking a *chillum*—the fundamental relationship to psychedelics in Buddhist practice and tradition is as intoxicants.

The precept in Theravadan Buddhism for dealing with intoxicants is one of the five basic training precepts: not to kill, not to steal, not to speak falsely, not to engage in sexual misconduct, and lastly, to refrain from using intoxicants to the point of heedlessness, loss of mindfulness, or loss of awareness. It does not say not to use them, and it is very explicit. It is interesting that it is worded that way: *to not use intoxicants to the point of loss of consciousness or awareness.* There is another translation of it, which says *not to use intoxicants which remove that sense of attention or awareness.* Then it is left up to the individual, as are all of the precepts, to use as a guideline to become more genuinely conscious.

A third thought I have to start the conversation, and I think I mention this in *Living Buddhist Masters,* is that practice in the West has taken a reverse direction from spiritual practice in the Asias, particularly Buddhist practice, but Hindu as well.

In Asia the tradition has three parts. You begin with *sila* or virtue. This is the foundation upon which any spiritual life is built. People take care with those precepts. They do not harm. There is a development of *ahimsa*, a respectful, caring, and nonviolent relationship to the people and beings around. This allows the heart to open and the mind to quiet. Out of *sila* comes the various spiritual practices. They are built on that as a foundation.

The second step comes after you are living a moral and a harmonious life—without which you cannot really have a quiet mind or an open heart. When your actions are in harmony, then you begin to train yourself through *yoga*, through concentration practices, through all different ways to begin to tame the wild and untamed monkey mind and to use that training to open up the inner realms. This is *samadhi*, or concentration.

The third domain is the domain of wisdom, *prajna*, from which arise the kinds of insights and understandings of the play of consciousness in the realm of human experience, based on the foundation of a moral life and the training in various disciplines. When those insights arise and wisdom comes they are established on a base so they become available to you easily. They *already* have become integrated in your life by your discipline and your prior training—and you have a context to understand them in. What has happened in the West seems to be a reverse of that.

Many people who took LSD, mushrooms, or whatever it was, along with a little spiritual reading of *The Tibetan Book of the Dead* or some Zen texts, had the gates of wisdom opened to a certain extent. They began to see that their limited consciousness was only one plane and one level and that there were a thousand new things to discover about the mind. There are many new realms, new perspectives on birth and death; on the nature of mind and consciousness as the field of creation, rather than the mechanical result of having a body, the biological result; and on the myth of separation and the truth of the oneness of things. Great kinds of wisdom opened up, and for some people, their hearts, too. They began to see the dance in much greater perspective.

People's obvious experience was that in order to maintain this they had to keep taking the psychedelics over and over; generally speaking, that is what happened. Even though there were some transformations from these experiences, they tended to fade for a lot of people, at least aspects of them. We might want to discuss this further.

Anyway, this is a kind of simplistic analogy to the East and West, but I think there might be some crucial points to it. Following that people said, "If we can't maintain the highs of consciousness that come through the psychedelics, let's see if there is some other way." And so people undertook various kinds of spiritual disciplines. They did *kundalini yoga* and *bastrika* breathing, or they did serious *hatha yoga* as a *sadhana, raja yoga*, light and concentration exercises, visualizations, or Buddhist practices as a way to get back to those profound and compelling states that had come through psychedelics.

RF: *Are you saying that it instilled in people a thirst for experiences?*

JK: A thirst, that is correct.

RF: *Is this the same thirst considered to be the cause of suffering in terms of the Buddha's second noble truth? Buddha taught that we suffer because of our desire or thirst for sensual or mental experience. Suffering is inevitable because everything is transitory, yet the thirst goes on. Even the highest mystical experiences can lead to suffering because of our tendency to become attached. In other words, I wonder if these experiences can actually inflate the ego or tempt it with the possibility that even "God" is within its grasp.*

JK: Well, the thirst has two sides to it. There is a useful thirst as well. When it is involved with a lot of grasping and attachment—to the extent that there is grasping and attachment—there is suffering. But psychedelics awakened in people not just a thirst, but a sense of the possibilities in exploring the mind and body and living in a different way. Then they began to have those sensitivities and those visions without repeatedly taking psychedelics, by undertaking some spiritual discipline, yoga, or meditation. People began to see that what was necessary was to take care with their speech, with their relationships, with their family, with their actions in the social community and the political world, in a way that was nonharming and that was conscious. So we have gone backward in a way to discover that the roots of fundamental change has to do with our physical body, with our behavior, and with all those things that are called "virtue," followed by a systematic discipline. Those are the supports for long-lasting or genuine access to these transformative experiences.

I would not say this is true for everyone. There may be people who actually have used psychedelics as a sadhana, as a practice. But I have been around a lot, and it is really rare.

RF: *LSD may be one of the most important causes for the importation of Eastern spiritual practices into this country during the 1960s. Because of LSD, as you are saying, young people sought out those maps and practices that could enable them to understand their experiences.*

JK: They certainly were powerful for me. I took LSD and other psychedelics at Dartmouth though I was studying Eastern thought even before then, but they came hand in hand as they did for many people. It is true for the majority of American Buddhist teachers that they had experience with psychedelics either right after they started their spiritual practice or prior to it.

I even know of cases where people were genuinely transformed by their experience in the way that one would be from an enlightenment experience. They are rare. Of the many hundreds of people I know who took psychedelics I know of a few cases where people had radically transformative experiences. These were as much as an "enlightenment" as any other kind of "initial enlightenment," using the terminology of a system that has a few major *satoris* and then finally full enlightenment. This is something you are welcome to print. However, along with it print that I am reluctant to say it because it may be misleading. It is like winning the lottery. There are not a lot of people that win. A lot of people play, and not so many people win. But the potential is there. I am not sure if it is helpful for people to hear that.

RF: *There is a story about a Buddhist master who was asked if you could use drugs to attain enlightenment. He paused and said, "I sure hope so." When Zen Master Soeng Sahn was asked what he thought about using drugs to help in the quest for self-knowledge he said, "Yes, there are special medicines which, if taken with the proper attitude, can facilitate self-realization." Then he added, "But if you have the proper attitude, you can take anything—take a walk, or a bath."*

Could you say more about sadhana? What is the right attitude? What are those qualities of mind and action that are basic to the Buddhist path?

JK: Okay, I am thinking if there is some linking question that comes in between these two. There is really. I will mention it briefly, and then I will go into the development of sadhana.

First of all, I have the utmost respect for the power of psychedelics. They are enormously powerful. They have inspired and opened and awakened possibilities in a lot of people in really deep ways. They have provided transformative experiences. In taking a tempered view of them it does not mean that I do not have a lot of respect for them and for the work that researchers like Stan Grof and others have done.

My sense from my own Buddhist practice and from the tradition as a teacher for many years is that people underestimate the kind of effort that is required to transform oneself in a spiritual practice. It requires a very great perspective called "a long enduring mind" by one Zen master, which means it can be days, weeks, months, years, and lifetimes. The propensities or conditioned habits that we have are so powerfully and deeply ingrained that even enormously compelling visions do not change them very much. Therefore, the system of liberation taught by the Buddha, and other great masters, draws on several different aspects or elements of life to help empower such a deep transformation. The Buddha said at one point, "Not good deeds, nor good karma, nor merit, nor rapture, nor visions, nor concentration, nor insight. None of these are the reasons I teach, but the sure heart's release, this and this alone." The possibility of human liberation is the center of his teachings. The liberation from greed, hatred, delusion, and the liberation from the sense of separateness and selfishness. This is a very compelling possibility for humans, and it is quite profound.

To come to this level of illumination, first one has to discover the power of those forces in the heart and mind that bind us. In the beginning it may sound like the forces of greed, hatred, and delusion are a little dislike of this and wanting of that, and not being so clear about things, being confused, or not seeing so deeply. But when you have undertaken a deep spiritual practice of whatever kind, and I will include psychedelic experiences as part of that, you begin to realize that what is meant is Greed with a capital G, the most primal kinds of grasping, and Hatred meaning Hitler and Attila the Hun in the mind, and Delusion meaning the deepest dark night. The forces are tremendously powerful. So then how does one encounter these forces and transform them in a way that leads to genuine liberation?

First, you have to have a lot of respect for them. And a lot of people use psychedelics in very misguided ways, with wrong understanding. Some modern researchers like Stan Grof have a much greater sense for set and setting and of the power of the forces that one can deal with. Similarly in spiritual practice one needs to respect the depth of these experiences. Secondly, one has to make a conscious commitment to the journey of spiritual change—through whatever inspiration: meeting an inspiring person, inspiring reading, faith, or through psychedelic experience.

Lama Chögyam Trungpa once spoke to a group in Berkeley and when he began he said, "My advice to you is not to undertake the spiritual path. It is too difficult, too long, and it is too demanding. What I would suggest, if you haven't already begun, is to go to the door, ask for your money back, and go home now." He said, "This is not a picnic. It is really going to ask everything of you, and you should understand that from the beginning. So it is best not to begin. However," he said, "if you do begin, it is best to finish."

For those who through some vision, faith, or reason have started, the next thing that is required, after seeing the power of these unconscious forces and of suffering in the world, is to make a commitment to the path of liberation, the path of the Bodhisattva, the path of the transformation of our being. To make that commitment wisely one has to realize that it encompasses every domain of life. This is the ground of spiritual discipline.

Spiritual discipline is based on our actions, our speech, and our relationship to people, animals, and plants in the environment. It is related to our inner thoughts, to whether our minds are filled with hatred, jealousy, and greed, or with kindness, tenderness, and compassion. It has to do with our intimate relations to our families, lovers, friends, and to the people we work with. All of this is a fundamental part of spiritual practice.

So there is seeing the forces, making a commitment to transformation, and seeing that the path is really a deep and fundamental one. There is realizing that the work of transformation takes place on all the levels of body, speech, and mind. Then there is the beginning of a spiritual sadhana.

Now your question comes in: What are the kinds of disciplines, what are the parts to it? Again, this is a kind of elaboration of what I started on.

The ground for systematic spiritual practice is virtue. Virtue doesn't mean commandments and/or moralistic teachings; it is an understanding that one have the proper—John Lilly would call it the "launching pad," or to have the earth base covered. And so one begins here.

Sadhana means to keep the five basic precepts in mind: not killing or harming living beings, not stealing, not taking that which isn't given—not being piggy basically in a world of limited resources. To use proper speech, that is, words that are both true and helpful—not brutal honesty—but to see that one's speech is both true and useful. Speech is very powerful. Words can heal. Many people have been healed by a word from their estranged father, a great teacher, even from a stranger in certain circumstances. And words have the power to create tremendous harm and to start wars. To refrain from sexual misconduct means to take care with the great power of sexual energy. Sexual energy can be associated with greed, compulsion, lust, denigration, exploitation, or it can be associated with intimacy, care, communion, attention, and love. So make sure that energy is used in a nonharming way. Finally for intoxicants: not to use intoxicants to the point of heedlessness, which means not use them to escape, to cover over one's pain or difficulty, or in a regular or addicted way in which one *has* to use them. There has been tremendous suffering in the lives of many millions of alcoholics, drug abusers, and great suffering for their families. The unnecessary pain, misuse, and widespread addiction to substances generally has been a concern of legitimate spiritual traditions for thousands of years.

Even among the relatively conscious explorers of contemporary psychedelics, addiction and attachment has sometimes been a problem. Even more critical is the overly positive message about both the spiritual and the casual use of these drugs that has been adopted by quite a few people who could not handle them well at all. As many of us who have used psychedelics have discovered, it is not an easy path. What matters from the point of view of this precept is to make their use nonhabitual (which probably means occasional). If one uses these substances, whether it is a glass of wine, a joint of marijuana, LSD, or mushrooms, this precept says to make that a conscious and careful part of your life. Without these precepts, if one even begins the journey, they will get lost or go off the track. You cannot complete the journey until you get the basics right. This is really a very simple message.

Almost every system in the world that is assisted by substances, including the wide range of shamanism, it is in a context of purification.

The purifications are first of action, which we talked about, that is, sila. Then based on that, there are the purifications of the body through hatha yoga, exercise, or practices that allow your body to feel and to be open enough to touch these deeper levels and to integrate them. You can take a very powerful substance, and even if you are physically a wreck, you can touch those places, but there will be a high physical price in the course of it. There will be the burning of the kundalini from the *nadis* opening much too quickly. When your body is in tune and open you can go to those places with much less of that burning and overwhelming physical disharmony that can come from it. Secondly, it allows the experience to be integrated. Without preparing the body one cannot hold those understandings. These are physical purifications of the body through diet, yoga, breathing, etc.

Then there are the purifications of the heart and mind, that is, emotions and thoughts. The purifications at the beginning are to train oneself to have thoughts of loving kindness and compassion. To begin, in a systematic way, to open up places that are constricted and extend forgiveness. This is the purification of forgiveness. There is an emotional transformation that takes place by extending forgiveness and opening the heart, seeing the fears, angers, and memories that have been locked in and releasing them.

There is the purification of generosity, of actions, words, and thoughts of caring. There is the purification in the realm of thought: taking the crazed monkey mind and nonstop inner dialogue and beginning to train the element of samadhi, or stability of mind. In this way, the mind becomes steadier and can focus on light, visualization, the heart, or some other aspect of being, instead of wandering all the time or being lost in the past and future.

It is necessary to begin to overcome the powerful conditioning of reacting with aversion to pain and with greed to pleasure, therefore getting lost all the time in past and future. This involves working with mindfulness and concentration in a specific systematic way. Then comes the mind, but first you stabilize the mind through concentration. Most people find that happens with a long regular practice of sitting meditation, with *mantra,* visualization, or a hundred other ways.

Once the mind is concentrated, you apply that one-pointedness to discover the laws of the mind or the laws of consciousness.

First you start on the level of greed, desire, fear, anger, laziness, or restlessness. These are the hindrances to transformation. You learn how to overcome them through your attention so that you do not become caught up or lost in them. You learn liberation in a very grounded way.

As your concentration builds and your body becomes more open and purified, you take that ability to be balanced and less caught by these energies to where you have access to other domains of consciousness, and you use that same ability in those other domains.

Now when you enter the domain of pure light filled with love and kindness, you have learned how to do that without getting too attached. You can see that too as part of the passing show. With the same attitude you go into the hell realms that arise through you. Not only is there greed or anger, but there is the deepest fear of dissolution in the realms of birth, death, and rebirth. You learn how to pay attention to those without so much grasping and attachment. This is where you learn not just the content of the various realms of consciousness, which the psychedelics can take you to, but how to relate to all of those wisely. If I were to put any sentence in the interview in capitals it would be to emphasize TO NOT JUST SEE THE CONTENT OF THE MANY REALMS OF HEART, MIND, AND BODY, BUT LEARN HOW TO RELATE TO THEIR CONTENT WISELY, COMPASSIONATELY, AND FREELY.

Most of the sadhanas require years of discipline. They require training under a competent master, because one is entering realms where it is almost a given that you will become attached, afraid, or go off course. You need a good guide and a systematic training in how to relate to pleasure and pain skillfully. One of the deepest roots of our conditioning that causes bondage is the fear and aversion of what is painful and the grasping and attachment to what is pleasant. And so we go through the rounds of *samsara,* which is repeating experience, over and over and over again.

Lama Chögyam Trungpa Rinpoche described it as a monkey jumping from window to window of a house. The windows being the eyes, ears, nose, tongue, sense of touch, and the mind—the six sense doors. From this one to that, liking this, disliking that, hopping from one window to another. Someone raised their hand and asked, "What happens if the monkey takes LSD?" Rinpoche said, "The monkey has already taken

LSD. So he experienced some new sights, sounds, tastes, and smells as a result of it—very powerful, compelling ones. He is still jumping around from window to window of the house because he hasn't learned to relate to those powerful and compelling visions in a wise way." He has not necessarily learned that from the visions alone, and as I said there may be a few exceptions. This is the point of view from systematic practice.

Suffering is caused by delusion and attachment, by grasping at anything that creates a sense of separation or sense of separate self. The fundamental liberation that is available is not some particular state, but is the liberation of not being caught by the different lights, by the ten thousand joys and the ten thousand sorrows that arise through the senses.

It takes sitting down and hanging out with difficult or blissful states over and over again, with pains in the body, fear, rapture, light, darkness, and learning how to bring a balanced attention, a steadiness of heart, and a greatness of heart to all of them. In this way it is possible to open to pain as the sorrow of the mother of the world and open to joy as the light of the sun. See both of them as our birthright and our inheritance and that neither of them is really who we are. This is an elaboration on your question of sadhana.

RF: *How can we understand the healing effect of psychedelic experience from the perspective of Buddhist psychology and meditation?*

JK: Healing takes place in a number of ways, but the most fundamental healing in Buddhist practice comes by bringing awareness to that which was twisted, knotted, or held in darkness in the body, feelings, thoughts, or in the domain of the views of mind. Through systematic meditation practice one brings the power of concentration and mindfulness to the knots, and the deepest patterns of tension open up. Without even doing a physical yoga, through sitting meditation, the deepest kinds of body work release occur. The places of emotional fear and holding from this life or any past lives will arise. The kinds of thoughts where we get attached, the opinions and views, and finally, the very deepest kind of holding on to our sense of self being separate, better, equal, or worse than someone else.

Healing with psychedelics is much the same. Healing comes when you have a suitable and careful situation and one's unconscious is opened by the psychedelics. Maybe they will relive a past trauma or experience the pain that is held in the physical body from an accident or an operation, or the tension from all their stored-up anger comes into consciousness and begins to release. The healing effects come through the power of bringing into consciousness that which has been below the threshold of consciousness. Part of the difficulty with psychedelics, and even with meditation at some points, is that it comes too quickly and people get overwhelmed. The danger is then they may shut down immediately afterward. They will touch a place that is too fearful or too difficult. But there are healings that take place in that way on all those levels of body, feelings, and mind.

RF: *They can be initiatory agents as well.*

JK: They can open the heart and show that we are not separate, that we can touch the realms of the universal, the *brahmavihara,* of universal loving kindness and universal compassion. They open the mind and reveal that consciousness and mind create the world, that the physical reality is created out of consciousness and not the opposite. They show that reality can be filled with light and humor. They can show that there are realms of tremendous transcendent understanding, that there are realms of many different time scales, eternally slow or eternally rapid. There are also realms of the *avici* hells where there is extraordinary pain and seemingly no way out.

RF: *Especially today in the West, where we have developed such mastery over the material world, something very powerful is required to show that this level is not the only one.*

JK: That is what Ram Dass says in part. He thought it was fitting that in such a materialistic era the expression of holiness should come in the form of a pill, in a materialistic form. I see them as definitely having been useful as an initial opening for people, and at certain stages it may be possible to use them wisely, again within the constraints of sila. They can be easily abused if one is not careful about the set and setting. This is something we are just experimenting with.

RF: *Maybe we could shift a little and discuss psychedelic substances in the history of Buddhism. What do you think of Gordon Wasson's article about the last meal of the Buddha being mushrooms (Wasson 1982)?*

JK: I have never read or heard of that in any of the mainline Buddhist traditions. In the *Pali Canon* Buddha ate not mushrooms but pork that had gone bad. In the *Mahayana Canon*, it was mushrooms because they are vegetarians. In the *Pali Canon* the Buddha took whatever was put in his begging bowl, whether it was meat or vegetable, as long as it was not killed for him. That statement that Wasson quotes from the *Digha Nikaya*, Buddha's last words before his meal:

> *I see no one, Cunda, on earth nor in Mara's heaven,*
> *nor in Brahma's heaven, among gods, and among men,*
> *whom, when he has eaten it, that food could be properly assimilated,*
> *save by a Tatagatha.*

This beautiful phrase is also said at other times in other sutras, not just when the food is bad. For example, there is a sutra where someone offers the Buddha a bowl of rice in a denigrated way and the Buddha says "no thank you." He will not receive it, and then he gives this exquisite sermon about what it means to be enlightened and that he does not need anything. The man's faith is fully restored, and he says to Buddha, "I give it to you now with tremendous good heart and faith." And the Buddha takes the bowl, and he says there is no one on earth who could eat this at this moment without it overwhelming them. So it really may be a symbolic statement.

RF: *It was a smith who served Buddha his last meal. This is an element that Wasson did not explore. In* The Forge and the Crucible, *Eliade (1978, 89) points out the connection between blacksmiths, alchemists, and*

shamans in India and elsewhere. He writes, "This relation between sha-
mans, heroes, and smiths is strongly supported in the epic poetry of central
Asia. Metalworkers almost everywhere form groups apart. They are myste-
rious beings who must be isolated from the rest of the community. Smiths
were thought to be masters of initiation, magical healers, shape shifters
and so on throughout the ancient world."

JK: It is interesting to look at Buddhist texts from the point of view of
world mythologies. I have not looked at that sutra in that way. Anyway,
in a simple way, there is not a lot that I have heard in any of the classic
traditions that speak to the use of psychedelic substances.

RF: *I wonder if they might be part of a body of secret teachings.*

JK: Like soma or other substances? Honestly, my guess is not. Not to
say that there might not be lamas in some corner of Tibet that have
some substance they use. Most likely it would be in the Tantric tradition, which is also more recent and more closely connected to Hindu
tantra which does use substances, at least modern Hindu tantra does.
But having been around a lot of the Buddhist world, it is not in my
experience yet, or in my knowledge. If it is secret, it is real secret. Most
of the lamas do not know about them either.

RF: *I have come across a couple possible psychedelic references in the*
Buddhist tradition. One that interests me I found quite accidentally
while looking for the Wasson article on Buddha's last meal. This arti-
cle is "Brewing and Drinking the Beer of Enlightenment in Tibetan
Buddhism," by John Ardussi (1977) of Australian National University. It
is a report on the ritual consumption of a beverage derived from grain that
inspired spiritual songs (doha) and deep mystical insight. Milarepa was an
initiate of this tradition. Although they repeatedly say "beer" in the article,
it must be an especially powerful beer to give rise to such experience. The
songs indicate that this beer was different from the usual chang *in Tibet.*
There may be an ergot fungus at work here.

Less psychedelic in terms of effects, but curiously related to the sub-

ject, is one of the incidents around the reincarnation of the Dalai Lama. After the thirteenth Dalai Lama died his body was seated on a throne facing south while lamas awaited signs for the arrival of his successor. The first sign was that the head mysteriously turned to face east. The second sign was the appearance of a large star-shaped fungus on a pillar also to the east, indicating the direction where the fourteenth Dalai Lama would take birth. This story is told by the Dalai Lama in his autobiography, My Land and My People *(1962). There is nothing to say that this fungus was psychedelic, but it is another auspicious association of fungi with worlds beyond the body.*

Could you say something about past lives?

JK: Past lives are a fundamental part of all the great Eastern teachings. There is a misunderstanding if one feels they are the owner of them, that it is "I" who lives this life and "I" who will live the next life. That is not correct. It is not reincarnation, but rebirth. It is like an apple seed being planted, turning into an apple tree, a blossom, a fruit, and then a new apple seed. This seed is not the same as the previous apple seed, but it is conditioned by it. It is like a match lighting a candle that lights a lantern. Each flame is conditioned by the previous one, yet each completely different in other ways.

Past lives are a basic part of the Buddhist teachings and most significantly are included in the description of the Buddha's own enlightenment. He had three visions called "the three watches of the night." In the first, he saw his own past lives, and he saw that it was a much bigger dance than he had ever imagined. In the second watch of the night he saw the birth and death of many beings according to the laws of karma and how ignorant they were of the laws that govern the process of death and rebirth. If they acted kindly, they were reborn in favorable circumstances; acting in hellish ways, they were reborn in hellish circumstances. In the third watch of the night he saw what binds beings to the wheel of birth and death in an unconscious way. It operates between lives, but also operates from day to day and from moment to moment in our lives. This is the law of dependent origination. Based on the senses and consciousness coming together and creating experience there is unskillful grasping at the pleasant, trying to hold on to ever-changing experiences, a resistance to the painful ones, and a sense of self through that.

Then he said, "I see a way out"—which is the way of equilibrium of heart and mind in which one takes the arising experiences and sees them as not self and does not grasp or resist them. Then he gave a whole systematic training that leads to human liberation and freedom.

So past and future lives are a big part of the Buddhist teaching, and all the realms that have come to light through psychedelic research are part of the Buddhist tradition: the archetypal realms, the heaven realms, the hell realms, the realm of the hungry ghosts, and so forth. There is nothing that I have seen in the realms that Grof and other modern psychedelic researchers describe that has not been charted by the breadth of Buddhist psychology. At the same time, Grof's cartography is comprehensive. It covers the research of modern psychedelics and describes most of the experiences that are traditionally written about in the context of Buddhist practices and attentional meditations. There is a great deal of overlap.

RF: *Why is it important to have rebirth as part of the Buddhist system?*

JK: It is not important. One can get liberated and come to great compassion and wisdom with no belief in past and future lives and no understanding of it. Birth and death actually take place moment to moment in this very life. You can experience the actual death and rebirth of the body and mind moment after moment in the deeper states of meditation, as you can through other ways, psychedelics included. It comes as a flashing out of nothing, into being, and then disappearance.

The closest modern analogy is of single pictures on a movie screen that appear to make a continuous living action but in fact are one moment after another of the arising of consciousness, the experience of the object with it, and then the passing away. You can come to see that all of life is a process of birth and death, moment to moment, through powerful training of the mind in concentration and intention.

RF: *Do you think it is possible to guide someone with psychedelics into that insight?*

JK: I am not sure that you can structure the psychedelic state so easily. It has its own laws of opening from what I have seen and from descriptions—as this meditation practice does. There are ways you can support it. In meditation you can tell people not to be attached or not to resist things, to sit quite still. Similarly for people who want to use psychedelics you could train them in meditation so they would learn not to be as identified, which gives them a certain power. You could create the proper set and setting, and you could remind them of it during the experience. But in terms of what material comes up, I do not think you have a lot of say about that in meditation or with psychedelics.

RF: *At a meeting held at the Harvard Divinity School in 1983, Dan Brown brought up the distinction between ecstasy and enstasis in a discussion about psychedelics. Ecstasy would be the flight of the soul from the body, "the soul's ecstatic journey through the various cosmic regions, whereas Yoga pursues enstasis, final concentration of the spirit, and escape from the cosmos" (Eliade 1964, 417). What do you think about this distinction with regard to psychedelic experience and meditation?*

JK: There is a very good article that Roland Fischer (1971) wrote while he was doing research at Johns Hopkins on the spectrum of ways of altering consciousness, from high stimulation to low stimulation. Buddhist meditation goes the route of enstasy to ecstasy. There exist ecstatic practices in Buddhist meditation, but primarily they work not so much by turning up the volume as by tuning the receiver—so you can receive what is going on in the unconscious and sensory level that is actually happening all the time. All these realms are available through more powerfully tuned awareness and concentration. Then you can get to realms where the body fills with light, you experience tremendous rapture and ecstasy, and are catapulted through all the realms of the heavens and hells.

I see psychedelics as one of the most fruitful areas of modern consciousness research. I would not be surprised if at some point there comes to be a useful marriage between some of these drugs and a systematic training or practice that I have described. That marriage will have to be based on an understanding of the ancient teachings, the laws of karma, responsibility, action, virtue, training the heart and the mind, and the laws of liberation.

One of the maps that is quite interesting from the Vipassana tradition is *The Progress of Insight* (Sayadaw 1978). One gains access to the progress of insight through the level of what is called access concentration, where thinking is pretty much stopped or slowed down. The mind can be steady on the object, the breath or wherever it is placed, through systematic training. I am not talking about years to do this, although to stabilize it in one's life it takes years. Some people can reach access concentration in ten days or two weeks in intensive meditation practice. Most others will take a year or so, but lots of people can reach it in ten days or two weeks. From access concentration you go through a process based on a finer and finer awareness and more and more precise looking into the body and mind. Here you begin to see parallels to Stan Grof's death-rebirth sequence of the four stages.

First there is simply a recognition of the interaction of body and mind, a seeing of its conditioned mechanical nature. This arises and that follows, sight arises and consciousness comes with it. Then feeling arises, then liking or disliking. You see the very mechanical workings of all which we take to be our self-experience. Following that, you begin to see how non-self it is. How, in fact, by being mechanical, our experience is all conditional and impermanent. Whatever our experience, it arises for a moment and passes away. None of it is graspable. There comes a deep insight into the characteristics of impermanence, ungraspability, insubstantiality, and *dukkha,* the unsatisfactory nature of it all. Then there comes a level of pseudo-nirvana, which Dan Goleman (1977) describes succinctly in his book, *Varieties of Meditation Experience*—the arising of dangerous states of rapture, awareness, equanimity, and light. It requires training to not become attached to these states. None of these are it. They are simply the beginning openings of the light of consciousness.

RF: *In* The Progress of Insight, *Mahasi Sayadaw lists these states under "corruptions of insight."*

JK: That is the translation, the corruptions of insight. Most people who have used psychedelics on their own have gotten lost at this place. It is a stick point, even in meditation with a good guide, and much more so in exploration with psychedelics. When one comes to the realization that none of those states are it (which is a profound insight), that you cannot attach to any of these as bringing liberation, then you start to observe these with detachment. That is the entry point into the deep process of death and rebirth that comes in the Vipassana tradition. The next stage is to see dissolution. Only after you have released those states of the mind and body filled with light, rapture, and equanimity, you see that everything, including those states, dissolves, and everywhere you look you see dissolution.

Based on that dissolution there arises tremendous fear. You look out the window, and the window is scary. You look at a someone, and you see they could die any minute. You look at your body, and there arise visions where pieces of the body fall off like hunks of meat. There are visions of many past lives that come at this stage, and all the ways that you have died before. There are visions of charnel grounds. The whole insecurity of life is revealed to you. Following this, based on dissolution and fear, there comes terror and misery, and you say, "I don't want any part of it, it is too scary." And you get caught for a moment, plopped into a new life, and forget all about it. And then some other dangerous thing happens, or you die again and want out.

Then there comes desire for deliverance, but it is so scary and so hard that at that point you say, "I can't do it. It is impossible. It is beyond me to let go that deeply. I want to go home." This is called the "roll up the mat stage," because you want to roll up your meditation mat and head home.

If you stay with it, finally there comes a full stabilization or balance of equanimity. It really requires a good guide because at the "roll up the mat" stage you do not believe you can go any further; it just seems impossible. Your teacher says, "Stay with it, just observe that, be aware with equanimity and balance." And finally, if you can observe even your desire for deliverance and you let go, there comes this state of tremendous detachment and presentness combined. This would parallel Grof's fourth stage. It is not a detachment of not caring. It is a perfect equanimity in the middle of experience that sees it all as empty and none of it as I, me, or mine. You see just arising and passing, and out of that, the deepest kinds of insights and enlightenment can come.

RF: *Do the Vipassana stages include visions of planetary annihilation?*

JK: The annihilation initially tends to be quite personal, and then it becomes as I said, universal. You see lifetime after lifetime. They could be planetary. I could imagine that arising.

RF: *I wanted to ask you about your feelings about where we are in the world, in terms of global ecology, politics?*

JK: I think about it often, and I talk about it to a lot of people. We should do everything we know how to educate people and transform our own hearts so that we learn to overcome the forces of greed, prejudice, and fear that start wars. If we cannot do it, how can we expect someone else to? We must use all the tools and disciplines, including the beneficial powers that may come through researching psychedelics. Certainly spiritual sadhana bears on the question of our planet. From the Buddhist point of view, one tries as best as possible, compassionately and passionately, to save all beings, plants, and animals—even though it is taught, and one can touch the realms in meditation where this is true, that there are world systems that come into being and pass away. Our *dharma* and our work is to bring as much of our heart and as much of our consciousness to this earth as we can. Whether it lasts or not, I do not know, and we will not know until we see, but the earth too is impermanent. All these things are impermanent.

RF: *Is there any mention of life on other planets in Buddhist teachings?*

JK: There is not much talk in terms of the meditation, but there are definitely writings on what are called world systems. It is said that the Buddha's mind was able to affect beings on tens of thousands of world systems.

RF: *Meaning actually physical places far, far away, as opposed to other-dimensional worlds?*

JK: Yes, physical places, and yes, that is in addition to all the realms of heaven and Brahma (which are different than heaven realms), hungry ghosts, *asuras,* and hell realms. There is as extensive a cosmology in Buddhism as anywhere that I have seen. There are equally extensive cosmologies—Egyptian, Sumerian, and shamanistic—but they are not quite as systematic.

RF: *Thank you for a most interesting talk.*

REFERENCES

Ardussi, J. "Brewing and Drinking the Beer of Enlightenment in Tibetan Buddhism." *Journal of the American Oriental Society* 97 (2) (1977).

Chah, A. In *A Still Forest Pool.* Edited by J. Kornfield and P. Breiter. Wheaton, Ill.: Theosophical Publishing House, 1985.

Dalai Lama. *My Land and My People.* New York: McGraw-Hill, 1962.

Eliade, M. *Yoga: Immortality and Freedom.* Princeton, N.J.: Bollingen Series, 1958.

———. *Shamanism: Archaic Techniques of Ecstasy.* Princeton, N.J.: Bollingen Series, 1964.

———. *The Forge and the Crucible.* Chicago: University of Chicago Press, 1978.

Fischer, R. "A Cartography of Ecstatic and Meditative States." *Science* 174 (1971): 897–904.

Goleman, D. *The Varieties of Meditation Experience.* New York: Putnam, 1977.

Govinda, Lama A. *Foundations of Tibetan Buddhism.* New York: Weiser, 1960.

Grof, S. *Realms of the Human Unconscious.* New York: E. P. Dutton, 1976.

Kornfield, J. *Living Buddhist Masters.* Boulder, Colo.: Prajna Press, 1977.

Lamb, B. *Wizard of the Upper Amazon.* Berkeley: North Atlantic Books, 1974.

Sayadaw, M. *The Progress of Insight.* Kandy, Sri Lanka: Buddhist Publication Society, 1978.

Smith, H. *Forgotten Truth.* New York: Harper and Row, 1976.

Wasson, G. "The Last Meal of the Buddha." *Journal of the American Oriental Society* 102 (4) (1982).

11 ACADEMIC AND RELIGIOUS FREEDOM IN THE STUDY OF THE MIND

Thomas B. Roberts

Thomas B. Roberts, who obtained his Ph.D. from Stanford University, investigates mind-body states for the leads they provide for learning, cognition, intelligence, creativity, mental health, psychological processes, and abilities that may reside in them as described in his book *Psychedelic Horizons*. He specializes in psychedelics, particularly their entheogenic (spiritual) uses; see *Psychoactive Sacramentals: Essays on Entheogens and Religion*. His online archive *Religion and Psychoactive Sacraments,* www.csp.org/chrestomathy, excerpts over 550 books, dissertations, and topical issues of journals. The two-volume set *Psychedelic Medicine* extends this interest into health studies. He has lectured on psychedelics in Finland, Iceland, the Czech Republic, Switzerland, Mexico, and Canada and published over one hundred articles, chapters, and book reviews. He is also the originator of Bicycle Day. www.cedu.niu.edu/lepf/edpsych/faculty/roberts/index_roberts.html.

ى

The attempts that have been made, during the last three hundred years, to grasp the psyche are all part and parcel of that tremendous expansion of knowledge that has brought the universe nearer to us in a way that staggers the imagination. The thousand-fold magnifications made possible by the electron microscope vie with the five hundred million light-year distances the telescope travels. Psychology is still a long way from a development similar to that which the other natural sciences have undergone; also, as we have seen, it has been much less able to shake off the trammels of philosophy. All the same, every science is a function of the psyche, and all knowledge is rooted in it. The psyche is the greatest of all cosmic wonders and is the sine qua non of the world as an object. It is in the highest degree odd that Western man, with but few—and ever fewer—exceptions, apparently pays so little regard to this fact. Swamped by the knowledge of external objects, the subject of all knowledge has been temporarily eclipsed to the point of seeming nonexistence.

C. G. JUNG, ON THE NATURE OF THE PSYCHE, 1946

WHEN LAWS FALL behind their culture what can we expect? In the general population we find extensive socially accepted lawlessness. In commerce new opportunities arise for those who cater to the newly rising illegal products and services. For the victims of the old laws, disrespect for the authorities who promulgated the mordant laws and for those who enforce them are the result. From those individuals and groups whose social, intellectual, spiritual, and moral standards are illegalized by the antiquated laws, we find feelings of resentment, alienation from the government, a lack of participation in community, and a distrust of political life. Anger arises from those whose lives are broken by enforcement of the antiquated laws.

From the viewpoint of the orthodox, established sectors of the culture the responses are frustration that the "old ways" are not being followed in the rising culture. Self-righteous anger and increased aggression against the lawbreakers are tinged with a holier-than-thou attitude. The new constituencies and minorities are blamed. A sense of confusion emerges over the defection of old friends and allies who have fallen into the clutches of the rising culture. They seem somehow treasonous, duped by underhanded tactics or their own naive ignorance. Paranoia.

With a special emphasis on psychedelics, this chapter describes some of the ideas, experiences, groups, and values that are victims of current drug law policies. These include the cognitive sciences, multistate psychology, religion, mystical experiences, and personal freedom. Drug policy decisions affect constituencies from these areas, and when new policies are written, these groups have a right to significant input into the reformulation of these policies and laws.

Most of the commentary on current drug policies comes from a narrow range of selected professional constituencies. By and large, parts of the legal, political, and medical communities dominate current discussions of rational alternatives to drug policies. These issues are also the responsibility of the academic, religious, and cognitive science communities; these groups have important stakes in the determination of drug policies, too.

THE MULTISTATE COGNITIVE SCIENCES

Cognitive science is a rapidly growing field that investigates mental processes such as perception, memory, thinking, and concept formation. Because all human action depends on these processes, cognitive studies goes right to the heart of what it means to be a human.

The Single-State Fallacy

To date most cognitive scientists have studied these processes almost exclusively as they take place in our ordinary awake state. But now a new, multistate perspective on our minds recognizes a broader direction: cognitive processes take place in all states. The outdated assumption that all worthwhile cognitive processes take place only in our ordinary awake state and that the processes in other states are worthless is called the single-state fallacy. Multistate cognitive science investigates cognition in all mind-body states (also called "states of consciousness" or "psychophysiological states"; Roberts 1989). Drug policy decisions are crucial to the future of multistate cognitive science. To appreciate why, it's helpful to know several things about this emerging field.

Multistate Mind

First, human cognition does take place in a huge variety of states, not just our usual awake state. Whether we are dreaming, asleep, awake, hyperexcited, deeply relaxed, concentrated or diffuse in our attention, alert to the outside world or inner directed, anesthetized, or even in a coma, cognitive processes continue. Each state has its own, special kinds of perception, memory, information-processing routines, and so forth, and each state organizes and orchestrates these capacities in distinctive ways.

From an information-processing perspective, a mind-body state is analogous to a software program. By increasing the number of programs we use in a computer, we expand our productive use of the computer. Similarly, by increasing the number of mind-body states we use, we increase the productivity of our minds. If we are to develop the most complete knowledge of human memory, perception, and thinking that we can, then we must explore these processes in as many states as we can. By needlessly restricting the accessibility of drug-produced states, current laws limit what we can know about our minds and how we can use them.

Psychotechnologies

Second, in their exploration of mind-body states, multistate cognitive psychologists use a large array of new and traditional psychotechnologies. These are methods of producing mind-body states. These include imagery, relaxation, many kinds of meditation, prayer and spiritual disciplines, the martial arts, yoga and body disciplines, breathing techniques, biofeedback, suggestion and hypnosis, near-death experiences, sensory overload and isolation, and others. Among the most important and diverse are psychoactive drugs.

Psychomagnifiers

Third, of particular importance to multistate cognitive science are the psychotechnologies that magnify weak mental processes, making them newly available for systematic, scientific, and scholarly observation. The impact of these psychomagnifiers for psychology and education is parallel to the impact of the microscope on biology and medicine. The most important of these is LSD.

While most drugs produce a more or less standard effect, LSD and the other psychedelics magnify perceptions of what is already going on in the mind, our cognitions. Because this amplification was not understood in the 1960s, the information lawmakers had about psychedelics was misleading, confusing, and incorrect, but our laws have not been updated to reflect scientific reality. In the politically charged atmosphere of the Vietnam War, racial unrest, and cultural revolution, it was easy to rationalize the political decision to outlaw these drugs as a public health decision.

Surveying the entire corpus of writings on psychedelics, Grinspoon and Bakalar (1979, 293) express the professional judgment of many of today's better-informed doctors, psychotherapists, scholars, scientists, and clergy:

> The interest is there, though stifled, and the problem is how to satisfy it safely and usefully. After more than ten years of almost total neglect, it is time to take up the work that was laid down unfinished in the sixties. We need to arrange a way for people to take psychedelic drugs responsibly under appropriate guidance within the law,

and a way for those who want to administer them to volunteers for therapeutic and general research to do so.

Evidence about the nature of the human mind may be the most significant information possible. Just as the magnifying power of the microscope made modern biology and medicine possible, the magnifying power of psychedelics offers to advance psychology and education into hitherto undreamed-of realms. Will new drug policies and laws facilitate cognitive exploration as a legitimate use of drugs, especially psychedelics?

Mental Research Tools

Fourth, the human mind is the primary research instrument; it is used in all research, scholarship, science, art, in every human endeavor. Everything we know comes from using our minds. What will we discover when we learn to use our minds in new ways, in new mind-body states, in new cognitive programs? The evidence from hypnosis, biofeedback, and meditation illustrates that we can develop additional useful physiological and cognitive capacities by accessing additional mind-body states. A multistate scholar, scientist, student, or researcher with access to many different states has a wider repertoire of cognitive resources than a single-state competitor who uses a narrow range of cognitive abilities. Current drug laws are a professional handicap. This applies equally to people working in every field: business, military, medicine, government, arts, religion, and so on.

Multiple Perspectives

Fifth, each mind-body state provides a unique perspective on itself and on other states. Meditative states, dreaming, and our usual awake state each teach us about each other as well as themselves. In addition to limiting the intellectual processes that the researcher can call on by restricting the number of states one can access, current laws limit the parts (programs) of the human mind that are open for study. This also limits the number of vantage points a researcher has for examining a specific capacity. Thus our current laws restrict our knowledge of mental processes such as perception, memory, problem solving, and creativity. Furthermore, our overall map of the human mind is incomplete when some mental lands are "off limits" to exploration. This is reminiscent of the fifteenth-century fear of sailing out into the ocean because you might fall off.

Practical Uses

Sixth, the many cognitive states of the human mind are more than just odd curiosities. Psychologists now realize that much valuable human thinking occurs in these states. Creative problem solving is noteworthy for taking place in altered states of consciousness. Psychotherapy can be sped up in some states, and exceptional performance sometimes results from such states. To develop the fullest range of human abilities, we need to develop ways of producing these states and learning how to use them. If we are to have a complete education, we must identify the worthwhile cognitive processes in these states and learn to use them.

ACADEMIC FREEDOM

Who has the right to determine what thoughts you may or may not think? Many Americans believe that they as individuals have the right to determine what goes on in their own minds, that thought control is not the right of a government. But an undesirable side effect of drug control is a kind of thought control.

Freedom of Cognition

I propose we recognize a new freedom. Freedom of cognition is the right to choose one's cognitive processes, to select how one will think, to recognize that the right to control thinking processes is the right of each individual person. In my own mind, I have little doubt that this is included in the Bill of Rights under freedom of the press, freedom of religion, freedom to assemble, the right to petition government, and other freedoms that vest the right to control one's own mind and thoughts with each individual citizen. Cognitive freedom is actually an extension of these freedoms, for the founders of this country certainly intended each citizen to exercise control over his or her own thought.

Our thinking is composed of both 1) the way we think (the cognitive processes we use and our skills in using them) and 2) the specific content of our thoughts (our ideas, concepts, assumptions, values, etc.). Freedom of thought includes freedom of both the contents of thinking and the processes of thinking. Self-control over one's own thoughts cannot occur if one does not have freedom to select both the specific ideas one finds truthful and the freedom to select the cognitive processes one uses when thinking with those ideas. Freedom of cognition includes selecting one's thinking process, one's mind-body state, provided, of course, it does no harm to others.

Today's governments that assume there is only one correct way of thinking (our ordinary awake cognitive program) are akin to past governments and churches that recognized only one correct thought or dogma. By and large, we do a good job recognizing and protecting freedom of content, but we do a weak job recognizing and protecting freedom of cognitive processes.

In the last fifty years a watershed has occurred in American culture and around the world. In this period, hundreds of millions of people discovered the enormous variety of psychotechnologies for producing mind-body states, cognitive programs. Some psychotechnologies come from other cultures, both ancient and modern. Other new ones were invented by the scientific advances of our time such as biofeedback and the newer psychoactive drugs.

These new and rediscovered psychotechnologies open up *a new kind of freedom,* which opposes an old kind of control. The right to select one's mind-body state is opposed by anachronistic laws from the single-state era. These laws may have been appropriate before the cognitive revolution when the single-state fallacy reigned, but recent advances in multistate research undermine the single-state theory and many of the anti-drug laws derived from it. The single-state assumption and its derivative laws now seem quaintly old-fashioned, a cultural artifact from a former era, contrary to scientific evidence and an impediment to the fullest future development of our minds

Double Censorship

By prohibiting access to certain states via its drug laws, our government is censoring the cognitive processes that reside in those states. It also indirectly censors ideas that are more credible in those states or to people who have experienced those states; the transcendent unity of all religions is an example of a disadvantaged idea. Current drug policies favor ideas that are more credible in our ordinary awake state. In former times governments, churches, and other powerful groups thought that seditious and heretical beliefs came from being exposed to harmful ideas in writing, speaking, or other forms of communication. They censored books. In our enlightened times, we recognize that heretical ideas also may come via direct experience. So we censor unorthodox experiences.

Handicapped Ideas

The claim that drug-induced experiences lead to ideas that might not otherwise be seriously considered is well illustrated in the lifetime works of R. Gordon Wasson. As a vice president of J. P. Morgan & Co., Wasson was hardly the stereotype of a '60s flower child. During their honeymoon in 1927, he and his Russian-born wife Valentina became interested in why some peoples are "mycophiles" and others "mycophobes." This resulted in their joint study of mushrooms as an intellectual hobby, but it did not result in any publications of scholarly or scientific note until after 1955 when Wasson discovered psychoactive mushrooms in Mexico. This experience so stimulated them that they (particularly R. Gordon Wasson) produced a steady stream of lively scholarly books on the probable influence of psychoactive plants on human culture, especially religion.

The Wassonian thesis that psychoactive plants played a major historical role in developing human cognition, philosophy, and religion makes eminently good sense to people who have been "bemushroomed," as Wasson called it. His broad intellectual scope and depth, his painstaking documentation, detailed analyses, and intriguing speculations rank among the richest contributions to the world of ideas made this century and are particularly notable as contributions by a nonacademic. These are documented in Riedlinger's book, *The Sacred Mushroom Seeker: Essays for R. Gordon Wasson* (1990).

Certainly any theologian, philosopher, Indologist, or anthropologist wanting to examine Wasson's claims should look at the best evidence, should ingest psychedelic mushrooms to see if his ideas are plausible. Because the use of drugs in academic and scholarly research is made illegal by current law, this method of intellectual inquiry is forbidden, and academic censorship is an unintended and unfortunate by-product of current policies.

Psychoactive drugs are important mind-body psychotechnologies, and laws that restrict drug abuse also damage the cognitive sciences and academic freedom. It is important to note that although some mind-body drugs may also have uses in medicine, from a multistate perspective both medical and nonmedical drugs are avenues for psychological and educational research.

FREEDOM OF RELIGION

Unitive consciousness—mystical experience. A major change in the Western psychology of religion during the last two decades is ignored by current drug laws. This is the reevaluation of states of unitive consciousness. Although this change is centered in the overlap among religion, psychology, and general culture, it also concerns areas of the arts, psychotherapy, anthropology, and related fields. In Western thought states of unitive consciousness are also known as mystical experiences, peak experiences, conversion states, intense religious experiences, cosmic consciousness, ego transcendence, and transcendent experiences. They also have a host of names in Eastern thought such as *samadhi, satori,* enlightenment, illumination, and so forth. Until the 1960s these states were generally considered to be evidence of neurosis or psychosis, and this error persists among professionals and laymen who are not familiar with the empirical research on them. Because some psychoactive drugs and other mind-body psychotechnologies can produce these states, they were erroneously thought to be psychologically damaging, and this error is reflected in our current drug policies.

Most of the time such states are likely to indicate psychological health rather than illness, and responsible social attitudes rather than irresponsibility. After he examined the evidence, Tart (1977) summarized the empirical findings: people who have had these experiences tend to be better educated, more successful, less racist, and happier on measures of psychological well-being. Supportive evidence continues to pile up (Wuthnow 1978; Noble 1987; Lukoff and Lu 1988): they also have more meaningful lives, less attachment to material possessions or to fame and power, less authoritarianism and dogmatism, higher ego strength, and are more imaginative, self-sufficient, intelligent, and relaxed. Walsh (1988, 549) lists the best researched psychotechnologies for producing unitive states:

> . . . the thought of harming "others" therefore makes no sense whatsoever. Rather, the natural expression of this state are said to be love and compassion or *agape*. Similar unitive experiences have been reported in the West among contemplatives (Wilber, Engler, and Brown 1986), subjects in exceptionally deep hypnotic states (Tart 1975), patients in advanced therapy (Bugental 1978), *experimental psychedelic sessions* (Grof 1988), and as spontaneous peak experiences (Walsh and Vaughan 1980). These experiences are under significant voluntary control only in contemplatives, either Eastern or Western, but interestingly, *enduring positive after effects on personality have been reported for all these conditions* and the approaches that induce

them have therefore been collectively named "holotropic therapies," i.e., growth toward wholeness (Grof 1988) or unity. [emphasis added]

Where is the recognition of this in drug policy? Nowhere. With their historical bias rooted in single-state ignorance and outdated assumptions about the human mind, our current policies, particularly toward psychedelics, are actually antitherapeutic, destructive of psychological growth, and antisocial. There have been over one thousand scientific research reports on psychedelics (Grinspoon and Bakalar 1979), yet our drug policies are uninformed of these and are, in fact, motivated more by manipulative fear-mongering politicians who use the tactic of scaring voters and then offering to save them from the fear they have created. Scientific, medical, religious, and psychotherapeutic evidence has no place in most state capitols or in Washington.

The Kingdom of Heaven Is within You

While Walsh concentrates on the psychotherapeutic aspects of unitive states, they are even more important from a religious perspective. Within all the world's major religious traditions, the direct experience of God (or the Absolute, the Sacred, the Ground of Being, or Cosmic Oneness) is seen as an essential stage of spiritual development. This occurs in states of unitive consciousness (Huxley 1945; James 1902; Smith 1976). Given the right set and setting, some illegal drugs (particularly LSD) can help facilitate these experiences. This is certainly not to say that all drugs always produce deep religious experience. Clearly this is not the case. But as Grinspoon and Bakalar (1979, 267) report, "It should not be necessary to supply any more proof that psychedelic drugs produce experiences that those who undergo them regard as religious in the fullest sense."

Government Control of Religious Education

I am one of these believers. In my life the most important steps in my spiritual development have occurred as a consequence of entheogenic sessions. The United States Congress, acting through the DEA and NIDA, has determined that I cannot practice the most important part of my religion in America. Most parents believe they have a sacred duty to nourish spiritual development in their children. To parents whose deepest spiritual experiences have been with entheogens, this means helping to make entheogenic experiences available to their mature children (probably in their late twenties or early thirties). Entheogens would be considered part of adult spiritual development, only to be taken voluntarily after becoming well informed. Although I know of parents who have guided their family members during entheogen sessions, it is probably preferable to have specially trained entheogenic practitioners who are not members of the family, to celebrate the sacrament only after extensive screening, to prepare the participants carefully, and to be located in a church-sponsored religious setting of natural beauty. I estimate that there are tens of thousands, perhaps hundreds of thousands of parents who desire to express their religious duty this way, but current drug laws undermine their parental spiritual responsibilities.

Within the theological and philosophical communities, there is disagreement about whether a drug-induced religious experience is a fake or genuine experience of unitive consciousness (Roberts and Hruby 1995). To those who believe it is genuinely sacred, banning the use of entheogens seems like a government-sponsored attack on their religions. Those who believe these are not genuinely sacred experiences use the power of governmental force to protect their religious assumptions, and governments at all levels are trapped into taking sides in a religious dispute. For those who are curious and would like to investigate the sacramental uses of psychoactive substances (entheogens) further, drug laws prohibit their investigations along this path of spiritual development.

Besides seeing entheogens as religiously 1) legitimate, 2) illegitimate, or 3) worth investigating, a fourth position also exists: whatever side one takes on the genuineness issue, the experiences can be educational. They may or may not be the "real thing," but as an approximation, they are valuable teaching-learning experiences. Just as pretend roads, stop signs, and traffic lights help kindergartners learn safety rules, simulated religious experiences give a taste of the genuine experience and can be valuable in religious education—better a rough approximation than complete ignorance.

But what if the approximation is not rough, but very close? What if it isn't an approximation but the genuine article? What is the truth? More entheogenic experimentation would provide evidence. No matter what side one takes on these issues, more knowledge will help clarify the answers; anyone who seriously cares about the answers to these questions—theologian, clergy, seminarian, layperson—should support the renewal of entheogenic research.

Do Americans really want the Office of National Drug Control Policy, Congress, the NIDA, the DEA, and their ilk to exercise control over religious sacraments, parental responsibilities, and religious education?

New Jerusalem vs. Armageddon

At the core of mystical experiences are powerful feelings of being united with God, all humanity, the world, and/or the cosmos, overpowering feelings of loving awe and goodness, and a sense of sacredness that stands behind and unites individual persons and objects. Grounded on such experiences, it is natural to find values based on a sense of unity in the universe; feelings of basic trust, security, belonging, and interrelatedness; beliefs in the innate goodness of human nature that in turn support the importance of relationships, cooperation, and community with all people; and stewardship rather than exploitation of God's world. All these express themselves in charity, compassion, and caring for others.

Among the likely characteristics of mystical experience are a sense of sacredness of all life and a desire to establish new, more harmonious relations with nature and with human beings. There is a corresponding renunciation of the various expressions of self-seeking, including the ethos of manipulation and control.

Mystical experience is manifest in a great many forms, some of which are of rather doubtful value. But only an empathic, self-forgetting mystical outlook, it could be argued, can restore to humankind the attitude toward life that will make possible its long-term survival. (Wulff 1991, 639)

When someone has experienced these feelings and gained these insights, natural reactions are: decreasing one's narcissistic sense of self-hood and preoccupation with personal salvation; feeling more secure in the world, less threatened by differences, and more inclusive toward others; and becoming more charitable and dedicated to working for the betterment of the world and humanity (Roberts 1995).

The Transcendentally Deprived

What if one hasn't had such an experience or what if one's religion denies or denigrates their existence? W. Smith (1988) claims that fundamentalism is the religious response to a waning sense of transcendence. To Shand's (1961) report that fundamentalist clergy had lower feelings of security and being "at-home" in the universe, Wulff (1991, 639) remarks, "The fundamentalists have presumably set their sights on heaven instead, and take the fate of the earth to be in God's hands." If Shand and Wulff are correct, then it becomes clear why opposition to social programs, concern with one's personal salvation, a disregard for society's future, a view of God as a punishing lawmaker rather than a loving parent, and laws against entheogens grow from the same anti-transcendental root.

Furthermore, if one assumes that human nature is basically depraved, then the last thing one would want to do is explore one's mind and magnify inherent human evils. Using Schacter's theory that emotion consists of two parts: 1) general arousal and 2) labeling or naming the arousal, Proudfoot (1985) proposes that the results of Pahnke's Good Friday Experiment (in which seminarians who took psilocybin experienced a sense of sacred mysticism during a church service) were due to how they labeled their experiences rather than the experience itself.

This is a central unresolved issue in the study of human nature as well as the psychology of religion. How much is in the experience, and how much is due to the way we label it? Certainly, seminarians attending a Good Friday service would be primed to interpret their experiences religiously.

If one believed that human nature was basically evil, that altered states weakened one's defenses against evil, that the Kingdom of God was not within, that the world was basically a frightening and dangerous place, then would psychedelic experiences magnify these expectations and produce a truly hellish trip? Perhaps entheogens are best left to members of transcendental denominations. On the other hand, would entheogens constitute religious enrichment for the transcendentally deprived? Looking at the chapters in this book, the answer looks like "yes." The issue is certainly much more complicated than this. Current laws foster religious ignorance, and we will never legally know. This situation illustrates how current laws blockade a frontier of religious exploration and impede the sacred search.

RECOMMENDATIONS

A major problem in drug policy (perhaps *the* major problem) is the fact that drugs have both medical and nonmedical uses. In this chapter, we have looked at the importance of drug policy for the cognitive sciences, religion, and academic freedom. Much of the current morass of drug laws is due to the fact that culturally legitimate but legally illegitimate, nonmedical uses of drugs are increasingly recognized by ordinary citizens, but not recognized by outdated laws. One reason for this is that most drug policies are made by the medical, political, legal, and law enforcement communities acting together and excluding other constituencies.

Drug laws are a peculiar institution. Within broad limits, we allow external freedoms such as freedom of the press and freedom of speech; these freedoms have to do with our outer, external behavior. But strangely, we regulate the freedom to select one's inner, mental, mind-body state, and it is even more personal, more individual, and more intimate than external freedoms.

It can hardly be expected that academic, religious, scientific, therapeutic, and intellectual communities will support laws that they see as contrary to their personal interests, interfering with professional standards and responsibilities, and against the public good. As more members of these groups come to understand the multistate aspects of human nature and recognize the single-state fallacy, they are likely to decrease their respect for existing drug laws. Thirty years ago when many of our drug laws were written, there was less popular recognition of the non-medical uses of drugs. Now that tens of millions of Americans readily accept both medical and nonmedical drugs, is it any wonder that disrespect for law and government are mushrooming?

Is there any path out of this morass? I think several national commissions would help. Each commission should address a particular area of drug use: religion, scholarship and the sciences, the arts, recreation, medicine, psychotherapy, and so on. The commissions should be staffed by experts in their respective fields.

Professional organizations should take the lead in examining how psychoactive drugs, especially psychomagnifiers, might contribute to their fields both as subjects of study and as techniques of doing research. Among the activities professional organizations should encourage are: organizing special interest groups, sponsoring sessions at professional meetings, publishing research on both the beneficial and destructive uses of drugs, and offering professional training for practitioners and researchers on how to use multiple states. Since most professional organizations see the furtherance of their profession as one of the tasks they undertake, it is a natural and easy step to extend professional development into a multistate perspective that includes both nondrug and drug ways of using our minds.

Likewise, drug policy should be examined in churches and religious groups, in schools and colleges, in civic organizations and the news media. Anyone who wants to see democracy work in America will welcome a frank, free, and open national discussion. What will the outcome of such a discussion be? One can never tell. But if we learn from history, psychoactive prohibition, like alcohol prohibition before it, will become such a political hot potato that the federal politicians will toss it to state governments, and we will see laws that take local customs and cultures into consideration. And as states learn from each other, eventually this is likely to gravitate toward common laws with small variations from state to state (Benjamin and Miller 1991).

American democracy is founded on the assumption that citizens have both a right to discuss laws and a duty to examine policies. Stifling debate on drug policy or any other topic and discouraging citizens from discussing the many alternative policies undermine this foundation of democracy. Public officials and private citizens who say that drug policy shouldn't even be debated are, quite bluntly, anti-American. Not only that, since drugs have been used sacramentally, they are anti-religious. And when they try to limit scholarly and scientific investigations of drugs, they are anti-science and anti-intellectual.

If prohibitionists truly believed that evidence and reason are on their side, they would enthusiastically encourage a national debate that would convince others of their claims. I have a feeling that those who want to prohibit discussion know the evidence is against them. Why else would they fear it? Their irrational fear of rational deliberation is tacit admission they are wrong, and know it. "Only error and wrong shun the light" (Wasson 1914, 4).

There are some difficult policy questions for professional organizations, national commissions, and private citizens to consider:

• Who has the right to determine what an American citizen can do with his or her own mind?
• Will the legal, governmental, and medical communities continue to monopolize drug laws?

- Will the right to determine one's own cognitive processes be recognized?
- Will academic freedom be restored in the cognitive sciences and elsewhere?
- Will freedom of religion be reestablished by allowing the use of entheogens for sacred purposes?
- Will psychotherapeutic effects of mystical experiences be considered?
- If the medical community reserves the right to determine drug usage for medical purposes, does the religious community have a parallel right for spiritual purposes? Will other professions enjoy similar rights?
- Can laws be written that allow beneficial nonmedical uses of drugs and at the same time discourage misuse?

We like to think that American liberty guarantees the right of the people to select their own ideas and ways of thinking; if we are to enjoy this freedom, then psychedelic-based ideas and psychedelic-supported cognitive skills need to be included, too. We like to see academic freedom as the freedom and duty to explore ideas wherever they may lead; if we are to continue this freedom, we must disregard the single-state fallacy and recognize intellectual development and scientific research in many mind-body states. We like to imagine that churches have responsibility for the spiritual development of their congregants; if we are to regain these rights, our laws need to accommodate churches that recognize the spiritual importance of entheogens. We like to believe that the U.S. Constitution enshrines freedom of religion, but the War on Drugs pries out this freedom, handing it over to the tyranny of the masses, embodied in the U.S. Congress; if we are to regain this freedom and the others above, we should support candidates who are realistic about drugs, who recognize that drug usage is more than a simple-minded good or bad.

It is time to consider both how to minimize harm and how to maximize benefits.

REFERENCES

Benjamin, D., and R. Miller. *Undoing Drugs: Beyond Legalization*. New York: Basic Books, 1991.

Bugental, J. *Psychotherapy and Process*. New York: Addison-Wesley, 1978.

Grinspoon, L., and J. Bakalar. *Psychedelic Drugs Reconsidered*. New York: Basic Books, 1979.

———. *Psychedelic Reflections*. New York: Human Sciences Press, 1983.

Grof, S. *The Adventure of Self-discovery*. Albany, N.Y.: State University of New York Press, 1988.

Huxley, A. *The Perennial Philosophy*. New York: Harper & Row, 1945.

James, W. *Varieties of Religious Experience*. New York: Modern Library, 1902, 1929.

Lukoff, D., and F. G. Lu. "Transpersonal Psychology Research Review, Topic: Mystical Experiences." *Journal of Transpersonal Psychology* 20 (4) (1988): 161–84.

Noble, K. D. "Psychological Health and the Experience of Transcendence." *The Counseling Psychologist* 15 (4) (1987): 601–14.

Proudfoot, W. *Religious Experience*. Berkeley: University of California Press, 1985.

Riedlinger, T. J., ed. *The Sacred Mushroom Seeker: Essays for R. Gordon Wasson*. Portland, Ore.: Dioscorides Press, 1990.

Roberts, T. B. "Multistate Education: Metacognitive Implications of the Mindbody Psychotechnologies." *Journal of Transpersonal Psychology* 21 (1) (1989): 83–102.

———. *States of Unitive Consciousness: Research Summary*. San Francisco: Council on Spiritual Practices (www.csp.org), 1995.

Roberts, T. B., and P. J. Hruby. *Religion and Psychoactive Sacraments: A Bibliographic Guide*. San Francisco: Council on Spiritual Practices (www.csp.org), 1995.

Shand, J. *A Factorial Analysis of Clergymen's Ratings of Concepts Regarding What It Means to Be Religious*. Ann Arbor, Mich.: University Microfilms, 1961.

Smith, H. *Forgotten Truth*. New York: E. P. Dutton, 1976.

Smith, W. "Transcendence: The Ingersoll Lecture." *Harvard Divinity School Bulletin* 18 (3) (1988): 10–15.

Tart, C. T. *States of Consciousness*. New York: E. P. Dutton, 1975.

———. *Psi: Scientific Studies of the Psychic Realm*. New York: E. P. Dutton, 1977.

Walsh, R. N. "Two Asian Psychologies and Their Implications for Western Psychologies." *American Journal of Psychotherapy* 42 (4) (1988): 543–60.

Walsh, R. N., and F. Vaughan. *Beyond Ego: Transpersonal Dimensions in Psychology*. Los Angeles: J. P. Tarcher, 1980.

Wasson, E. A. *Religion and Drink*. New York: Burr Publishing House, 1914.

Wilber, K., J. Engler, and D. Brown, eds. *Transformations of Consciousness: Conventional and Contemplative Perspectives on Development*. Boston: Shambhala, 1986.

Wulff, D. *Psychology of Religion: Classic and Contemporary Views*. New York: John Wiley and Sons, 1991.

Wuthnow, R. "Peak Experiences: Some Empirical Tests." *Journal of Humanistic Psychology* 18 (3) (1978): 59–75.

12 BIOMEDICAL RESEARCH WITH PSYCHEDELICS

Current Models and Future Prospects

Rick J. Strassman

Rick Strassman, M.D., performed the first new human studies with psychedelic drugs in the United States in over twenty years. His research involved the powerful, naturally occurring compound DMT—N,N-dimethyltryptamine. He wrote about this research in the popular book *DMT: The Spirit Molecule,* now in its fifteenth printing. With three distinguished collaborators, he coauthored *Inner Paths to Outer Space,* which looks more carefully at the common "other worlds" experience that volunteers frequently reported during his research. Dr. Strassman is currently clinical associate professor of psychiatry at the University of New Mexico School of Medicine. He is also president and cofounder of the Cottonwood Research Foundation, http://cottonwoodresearch.org, which is dedicated to consciousness research. www.rickstrassman.com.

LSD was the beginning of a new era. I once called it a "mind craft of the Noosphere" (Teillard de Chardin's word). Psychedelics are instruments and like most of our artifacts are capable of being used well or ill. Unluckily misuse is at least as likely as good use. However there is plenty of evidence that LSD and other psychedelics can be used well provided one recognizes that we have to make the necessary effort to use them well in any particular setting. Time, effort, and imagination is needed. So far we have been unwilling to make the necessary effort. Too few people have had the necessary imagination to understand the nature of Albert Hofmann's gift to his fellow creatures. Of course this has been the usual fate of great discoveries. Both the telescope and the microscope began their careers as more or less amusing toys. Both of them seemed at first so crude that many astronomers and anatomists doubted whether they could be of any use to science. Both of them had for many years serious limitations. Both of them produced serious distortions which for years disqualified them as scientific instruments. . . . There were all kinds of instrument errors which have been gradually corrected over the years. . . .

HUMPHRY OSMOND, LETTER TO BETTY EISNER AT
THE SWISS MEDICAL ACADEMY CONFERENCE
COMMEMORATING FIFTY YEARS OF LSD, 1993

THE FIRST STAGE of renewed human medical research with psychedelics is ending (Strassman 1995). This chapter will present the important accomplishments and how these will shape the development of future human studies. As medicine, science, and religion enter the next millennium of the Christian era, it also is a good time to consider how best to assess the religious or spiritual aspects of the psychedelic experience.

These particular areas should not be ignored in our scientific study for they may provide the most unique and important data.

The first evidence for the resurgence of government-sanctioned human research with highly restricted "classical" psychedelics was a paper published in the late 1980s by German psychiatric researchers describing human responses to mescaline (Oepen et al. 1989). Since then, they have also performed projects with MDMA ("X," "ecstasy"), MDE (a chemical relative of MDMA), and psilocybin. In addition to the German studies, Swiss scientists began, at about the same time, human research with LSD, MDMA, psilocybin, and ketamine (Vollenweider 1994).

New North American human research began in 1990 at the University of New Mexico with DMT, a short-acting tryptamine hallucinogen found in many plants and animals, including humans (Strassman 1991). Subsequently, human studies began with psilocybin in New Mexico, ibogaine (an African hallucinogen) at the University of Miami, and MDMA at UCLA. Human ketamine research has been taking place in Russia for several years (Krupitsky et al. 1995), and is now also occurring at Yale (Krystal et al. 1994), the National Institute on Drug Abuse, and the University of Washington. Data from field research undertaken in Brazil on the effects of taking ayahuasca (containing DMT) in a religious context have also been published (Grob et al. 1996).

These psychedelic drugs are all, except for ketamine, in the most restricted of categories established by governmental legislation and regulations. Severe penalties exist for making, possessing, using, or distributing them. The legislation and its implementation, in the early 1970s, resulted in a generation of neglect of peer-reviewed human psychedelic research. This research showed promise in understanding human mind-brain relationships and in treating intractable psychiatric conditions, including alcoholism and drug abuse (Kurland et al. 1967; Albaugh and Anderson 1974) and the terminally ill. Despite being so tightly regulated, psychedelics continue being used in illicit, nonmedical ways that attract a great deal of negative and positive attention. The promising research, historical, and ethnographic literature about these drugs contrasts sharply with most media and educational condemnation of them and is a good example of a curious dichotomy within our society.

The sociopolitical pressures on the performance of this research are thus unusually overt. Those now performing it received their training during this void in medical investigation of the psychedelics, aware that the strong resistance to any use of psychedelics resulted in this hiatus. These factors may explain the particular approach taken in initiating a renewal of the field.

This first stage of research has been primarily focused on biological effects of these drugs, with less emphasis on effects on consciousness and spiritual/religious issues. The only exception was the Swiss psychotherapy protocol using LSD and MDMA, from which, to date, we unfortunately have few data.

The emphasis on physical effects of psychedelics is routine in the earliest, or Phase I, studies of any new compound intended for medical use. In the case of psychedelics, it has been important to once more establish a solid safety record in humans. This was generally accepted early in the history of psychiatric research with psychedelics, starting in the 1940s. However, implicit in the lack of ongoing studies for so long was the necessity to again show regulatory boards that under careful supervision, psychedelics could be given to people safely. Results from current research have reaffirmed this view (Strassman and Qualls 1994; Strassman et al. 1994). Much has been written about psychiatric adverse effects of psychedelics (Strassman 1984). The most comprehensive reviews suggest that in well-screened, prepared, supervised, and followed-up psychiatric patients taking pure psychedelic drugs, the incidence of serious adverse reactions is less than 1 percent. It is even lower in "normal volunteers." Those most likely to suffer from prolonged depression, anxiety, or psychotic reactions to psychedelics are usually those with pre-existing psychiatric disorders, taking drugs of uncertain dose, nature, and quality, usually in combination with other drugs and alcohol, in an uncontrolled setting.

More subtle adverse effects, however, are of interest to proponents of the nonmedical use of psychedelics. These include a feeling of superiority in those who have taken a psychedelic over those who have not. Rather than increasing tolerance for differences and compassion for those who may (or may not) be less spiritually or personally developed than oneself, this seems a move backward, by increasing judgmentalism and divisiveness.

Another rarely discussed adverse effect of nonmedical psychedelic use is the belief that coming to a particular understanding or resolution of a personal problem on a psychedelic trip is the same as living the understanding or resolution in daily life. We have all seen people who had deep, moving, and profound "Ah, ha!" experiences on psychedelics, resolving thorny issues. However, once they "come down," they no longer consciously are working on applying what they saw, felt, and worked though while "high." In these cases, never having taken a psychedelic to work on the problem (and attain some ephemeral solution) might have forced them to work on it more steadfastly, consistently, and effectively. The illusory solution found on a psychedelic may turn out to be worse than no solution by virtue of believing things have changed, when they have not in actual practice.

Traditionally, the next step in bringing a drug into common medical practice is to perform Phase II studies, in which small numbers of patients with a particular disease are treated. If these results are promising, large-scale, multisite Phase III projects then take place. Finally, a New Drug Application is submitted to the Food and Drug Administration for permission to begin selling the drug for use in one or more disorders. Since the typical psychedelics have been in existence for so long, there is no patent on the drugs themselves, although their use has been patented in certain circumstances. Thus, unless a drug company invented a new psychedelic drug, there is no incentive for the pharmaceutical industry to spend the time and money performing any of the studies necessary for psychedelics to enter the mainstream medical repertoire of drugs.

This issue of applicability of using psychedelics for purposes other than treating a clear pathology will become highly focused if research continues with these drugs for much longer. The multimillion-dollar drug study to test, for example, a new anti-depressant in hundreds of patients is an unlikely model for assessing the usefulness of psychedelics in dealing with more subtle problems, such as creativity enhancement (Harman et al. 1966) and deepening religious practice and commitment.

An opportunity exists for novel research to take place within the context of religious use of psychedelics. Certain religious groups, not driven by the same forces as the pharmaceutical industry and traditional medical (profit and therapy, respectively), are using psychedelics as "highly active sacraments." These include the Native American Church and the Brazilian ayahuasca-using churches. Applying modified psychiatric research analytic methods to the use of these drugs in these unique settings could be a fruitful cross-fertilization and collaboration between science and religion.

Similar to research a generation ago, different groups use different labels for these drugs, ranging from "psychedelic," to "psychotomimetic," to "entheogenic." As "set" and "setting," the internal and external circumstances in which a psychedelic is given or taken, are of such importance to the nature of the subjective response, how these drugs are considered is of great importance to the type of drug reactions seen and the researchers' response to them. My preference is "psychedelic," as it avoids the "saintly" or "schizophrenic" poles that might implicitly or explicitly constrain the broad spectrum of effects possible with these agents.

It will be of interest to note how research centers' use of terminology for psychedelic drugs affects reporting of adverse effects. For example, would those research teams with a "psychotomimetic" approach report more adverse reactions than those adopting an "entheogenic" perspective? Would the latter team's tolerance for unusual states allow difficult reactions in experiments to work themselves through, as opposed to labeling and treating as pathological the same condition in a different research paradigm? In addition, learning how participants and leaders of traditional psychedelic religious ceremonies label and manage "adverse effects" could add an extra dimension to our theoretical and practical understanding of the range of psychedelic responses.

Based on our experience giving high doses of DMT to psychedelic-experienced normal volunteers, I think that psychedelics chemically change the tuning, or receiving characteristics, of the brain. The totality of potential information received by both the "normal" and "psychedelicized" brain is, of course, greater than "either" brain can consciously take in.

The most interesting extension of this is that one might be able to perceive normally "invisible things." These could include personal memories, thoughts, and feelings that are normally barely, if at all, conscious. Thus, psychological effects can predominate in certain circumstances, particularly with lower doses of psychedelics.

This novel information may also "reside" in nonmaterial states. Current evidence suggests that over 95 percent of matter in the universe is "dark," or "invisible," only perceived by its indirect effects. Perhaps with a change in receiving properties, the brain, and its mind, are now able to perceive additional amounts of information. This train of thought might be seen as a logical extension and development of Aldous Huxley's coining of the concept of the brain's function being largely one of a "reducing valve" (Huxley 1954) and fleshes out Hofmann's suggestion that psychedelics alter brain receiving characteristics (Hofmann 1983).

In our New Mexico DMT research, I was faced with the choice of how best to help our volunteers understand the nature of their DMT experiences. For many, a high dose of intravenous DMT produced the most intense, moving, and novel psychedelic sessions of their lives, with deep meaning and (at least short-term) impact.

"Explaining" what they had just undergone by invoking only serotonin receptor function changes in brain sites did an injustice to the depth of their experience. "Yes," they would reply, "but what about what

I just saw and felt? Are there brain centers for clowns, elves, and aliens? Where did this really come from?"

By conceiving of the brain as a receiver for information, however, one can accommodate the biological model of changing brain function with a chemical. At the same time, it allows for the possibility that what is being received, while not usually perceptible, is consistently and verifiably existent for a large number of individuals. It may, indeed, reflect stable, freestanding, and parallel planes of reality.

BIRTH, DEATH, NEAR DEATH, AND ABDUCTIONS

We can suggest further areas of research that partake of more speculative realms, which are still within, but stretch the bounds of, scientific study. These are suggested by the presence of DMT in the human body. The function of DMT in our bodies is unknown, but levels in psychotic patients fluctuate with intensity of psychotic symptoms, such as hallucinations (Rodnight et al. 1976). In rodents, it has been shown that DMT exists in the brain at birth (Beaton and Morris 1984) and also increases with stress (Barker, Monti, and Christian 1981).

It is possible that the human brain synthesizes and releases large quantities of DMT during especially stressful psychophysical states. The pineal gland has the highest levels of the DMT precursor serotonin anywhere in the brain, and it may be a preferential site of DMT synthesis. However, any brain site with serotonin, or another DMT precursor, tryptamine, might also produce DMT under certain circumstances.

There is appeal in invoking a role for the pineal because of its developmental schedule in the human fetus. This light-sensitive organ does not develop in the human until forty-nine days after conception. The forty-nine-day period also is how long the Tibetan Buddhist Book of the Dead and other traditions suggest the life force of an individual remains free-ranging, as it were, before coalescing around another distinct individual physical form. The fetal reproductive organs do not take shape as either male or female until forty-nine days postconception, too.

One could tie into a nice "metaphysical" knot the triad of "spirit," "sex," and "individuality." In this scenario, the unique life force of a person enters through the pineal, affecting its function metabolically, releasing DMT into the fetus. The fetus is only able to attract or absorb this life force when it is ready: male or female gender decided, a metabolic source of DMT now available. The stress of childbirth also may stimulate DMT production. So, this fetal and birth-related DMT release could set the template for re-experiencing additional episodes of elevated DMT levels during other highly stressful conditions. These could include starvation, fever, and lack of oxygen, alone or in combination, resulting in a near-death experience (NDE). As well, prolonged meditation might possibly trigger excess DMT synthesis. Later, at death, the emptying of the life force out of the body may take place via the pineal, too, once more releasing copious amounts of DMT as the metabolic result of this movement of life energy.

If this were the case, then those who have had an NDE could be given DMT and drug effects compared to the naturally occurring NDE. Many of our DMT volunteers said that they were no longer afraid of death and that they believed that DMT would be a good drug to use as a "dry-run" of the dying process. In addition, levels of DMT in the newly dead could be measured, although the ethical and informed consent concerns of this type of postmortem research may be problematic.

In addition, some of the "UFO encounters" reported in the popular literature sound very similar to some of our DMT volunteers' reports of their high-dose sessions, even those who had little familiarity or interest in "abduction" phenomena. Contact with "aliens," being experimented on in highly technological settings, implantation of devices, and transmission of information all were seen in our DMT work. In a similar vein, perhaps "nondrug" abductees were in a highly stressful situation, giving rise to the production of high levels of DMT naturally. Administering DMT to abductees and comparing the phenomenology of their reports could shed light on the basis of abduction phenomena.

This line of thinking usually gives rise to questions about the evolutionary significance of DMT being synthesized in the human body. "Why do we all have DMT in our brains?" "Why is there a compound that when given (or produced) generates experiences of 'alien contact,' death, space travel, and other extraordinary effects?" However, the comparable question is not asked of silicon in computer chips. Rather, silicon is in computer chips because it works; it's the best molecule for the function needed. In the same way, we have DMT in our brains because it works. It's the best molecule for the function needed, to retune the perceiving abilities of the brain to different levels.

RELIGIOUS IMPLICATIONS

The highly speculative nature of these musings leads, naturally, to thoughts about heaven, hell, the afterlife, the soul, reincarnation and transmigration, life, death, and the meaning of existence. At least they do in me! Although I am predisposed to such intellectual roaming, I do not think there is much intrinsic merit to either hypothesizing or proving the hypotheses put forth. This is the point at which perhaps the most dangerous aspect of the psychedelic experience, its potential to provide unbalanced wisdom, insight, and enlightenment, is exposed and then converted to a better use. That is, "spiritual experience" alone, even repeated, is not the basis of becoming a better or more useful person. Rather, psychedelic insights tempered and put into practice using ethical and moral considerations appears the best way to harness the power of psychedelic drugs.

I have so far avoided defining "spiritual" or "religious." That is because it is not common practice to do so. Are things spiritual because they are not perceived with the five senses, that is, "nonmaterial"? Or, are they spiritual because they feel so good, or so bad? On the other hand, are things religious because of their impact on human behavior—

becoming more loving, tolerant, kind, and sympathetic and less greedy, warlike, destructive, and thoughtless?

There are kind, compassionate, helpful people who have never had a "spiritual" experience, drug-induced or otherwise. And, I've seen people with numerous drug-induced "enlightenment" experiences who excessively indulge in all manner of disrespectful, destructive behavior.

As the theme of this book suggests, there is hope that somehow there can be an infusion of moral, ethical, and ultimately practical influence into the outcomes of the full psychedelic experience. This is so that those who desire further experiences with nonordinary realities, or deeper personal therapeutic ones, can do so in the most constructive way possible.

TRAINING ISSUES

Regardless of the explicit research or other context for administering psychedelics to humans, I believe certain qualifications should be met. One of the more controversial is that of "self-experimentation."

Before the 1960s, self-experimentation was a generally recognized tool in psychopharmacology (Szara 1957). Current European psychedelic researchers are required to "go first" in their studies. This is for safety issues and to increase the quality of informed consent provided by the investigator (F. X. Vollenweider, pers. comm.; L. Hermle, pers. comm.). It also provides pilot data for further refinement of hypotheses and techniques and enhanced empathy with volunteers' experiences. Future North American studies should request permission from regulatory boards to follow our European colleagues in this extraordinarily important matter.

In addition to "having been there oneself," one who plans on administering psychedelics to others must clearly examine his or her motivations to do so. Are there nontherapeutic or otherwise masked reasons behind this decision? Controlling or sadistic urges? A depression that may be lifted by the admiration and love of a psychedelic-intoxicated person in a helpless and dependent position? Particular sexual fantasies attached to one's goals? Possessing and using a magic bullet to solve the ills of the world, in a way not possible within a frustrating and painful childhood? Formal training in self-examination ought to be required for anyone in such a powerful position as giving psychedelics to people.

I believe psychoanalytic psychotherapy or psychoanalysis provides a thorough and comprehensive system in which to do this work. The importance of childhood experiences, parenting styles, acceptance of unconscious motivations and drives affecting our behavior and feelings, reliving of regressive relationships in the presence of the therapist—all these can be extremely useful in looking at one's motivations for any work or relationship. This is even more important if one is to make a living by administering psychedelics.

Finally, understanding religious sensibilities in as deep a manner as possible is necessary for being able to absorb and work with some of the most difficult and complex material brought up in psychedelic sessions. This does not only mean having deep "spiritual" or "religious" experiences oneself, with or without a psychedelic. Rather, there ought to be training and background in religious practice, of whatever sort.

For me, Buddhism provided this religious context within which I could hold, understand, and build upon the psychedelic sessions we encountered in New Mexico (Strassman 1996). A solid sitting meditation practice helped me stay alert, interested, nonintrusive, and available to respond to volunteers when needed. Buddhism's acknowledgment and acceptance of, but practical approach to, "denizens" of nonmaterial realms also helped me deal directly with the meaning and implications of people's encounters with these inhabitants of usually unseen worlds. The themes of death, impermanence, and loss of self-image seen with high doses of DMT also could be held, looked at, and worked on within the Buddhist framework. Finally, the ethical and moral structure of Buddhism, based as it is upon a particularly wide view of reality, was of help in directing people toward where to take what they had learned on their high-dose DMT sessions.

In terms of combining religious practice and psychedelic drugs in a fruitful way, one simple model comes to mind. This is one in which a religious aspirant, with strong moral and intellectual understanding of religious doctrine, practice, and community, lacks a deep experiential realization of the bases of these doctrines and practices. The view provided by a properly prepared, supervised, and followed-up high-dose psychedelic experience may provide the validation of the teachings necessary for inspiration to continue the work at hand.

The flow of information should be in both directions. That is, the adoption and practice of ethical and moral guidelines from the great religious traditions should be used to enhance the effectiveness and utility of the giving and taking of psychedelics in all circumstances.

REFERENCES

Abraham, H. D., and A. M. Aldridge. "Adverse Consequences of Lysergic Acid Diethylamide." *Addiction* 88 (1993): 1327–34.

Albaugh, B. J., and P. O. Anderson. "Peyote in the Treatment of Alcoholism among American Indians." *American Journal of Psychiatry* 131 (1974): 1247–51.

Barker, S. A., J. A. Monti, and S. T. Christian. "N,N-Dimethyltryptamine: An Endogenous Hallucinogen." *International Review of Neurobiology* 22 (1981): 83–110.

Beaton, J. M., and P. E. Morris. "Ontogeny of N,N-dimethyltryptamine and Related Indolealkylamine Levels in Neonatal Rats." *Mechanisms of Ageing and Development* 25 (1984): 343–47.

Dittrich, A., S. von Arx, and S. Staub. "International Study on Altered States of Consciousness (ISASC) Summary of the Results." *German Journal of Psychology* 9 (1985): 319–39.

Grob, C. S., D. J. McKenna, J. C. Callaway, et al. "Human Psychopharmacology of Hoasca, a Plant Hallucinogen Used in Ritual Context in Brazil." *Journal of Nervous and Mental Disease* 184 (1996): 86–94.

Harman, W. W., R. H. McKim, R. E. Mogar, et al. "Psychedelic Agents in Creative Problem-Solving: A Pilot Study." *Psychological Reports* 19 (1966): 211–27.

Hofmann, A. *LSD: My Problem Child.* Los Angeles: J. P. Tarcher, 1983.

Huxley, A. *The Doors of Perception.* New York: Harper and Row, 1954.

Krupitsky, E. M., V. B. Ivanov, L. S. Priputina, et al. "The Combination of Psychedelic and Aversive Approaches in Alcoholism Treatment: The Affective Contra-attribution Method." *Alcoholism Treatment Quarterly* 9 (1995): 99–105.

Krystal, J. H., L. P. Karper, J. P. Seibyl, et al. "Subanesthetic Effects of the Noncompetitive NMDA Antagonist, Ketamine, in Humans. Psychotomimetic, Perceptual, Cognitive, and Neuroendocrine Responses." *Archives of General Psychiatry* 51 (1994): 199–214.

Kurland, A. A., S. Unger, J. W. Shaffer, et al. "Psychedelic Therapy Using LSD in the Treatment of the Alcoholic Patient: A Preliminary Report." *American Journal of Psychiatry* 123 (1967): 1202–9.

Oepen, G., M. Fuengeld, A. Harrington, et al. "Right Hemisphere Involvement in Mescaline-induced Psychosis." *Psychiatry Research* 29 (1989): 335–36.

Olfson, M., and H. A. Pincus. "Outpatient Psychotherapy in the United States, I: Volume, Costs, and User Characteristics." *American Journal of Psychiatry* 151 (9) (1994):1281–88.

Pahnke, W. N., A. A. Kurland, S. Unger, et al. "The Experimental Use of Psychedelic (LSD) Psychotherapy." *Journal of the American Medical Association* 212 (1970): 1856–63.

Rodnight, R., R. M. Murray, M. C. H. Oon, et al. "Urinary Dimethyltryptamine and Psychiatric Symptomatology and Classification." *Psychological Medicine* 6 (1976): 649–57.

Strassman, R. J. "Adverse Reactions to Psychedelic Drugs. A Review of the Literature." *Journal of Nervous and Mental Disease* 172 (1984): 577–95.

———. "Human Hallucinogenic Drug Research in the United States: A Present-day Case History and Review of the Process." *Journal of Psychoactive Drugs* 23 (1991): 29–38.

———. "Hallucinogenic Drugs in Psychiatric Research and Treatment: Perspectives and Prospects." *Journal of Nervous and Mental Disease* 183 (1995): 127–38.

———. "DMT and the Dharma." *Tricycle: The Buddhist Review* 6 (1) (1996 Fall).

Strassman, R. J., and C. R. Qualls. "Dose-response Study of N,N-dimethyltryptamine in Humans. I: Neuroendocrine, Autonomic, and Cardiovascular Effects." *Archives of General Psychiatry* 51 (1994): 85–97.

Strassman, R. J., C. R. Qualls, E. H. Uhlenhuth, et al. "Dose-response Study of N,N-dimethyltryptamine in Humans. II: Subjective Effects and Preliminary Results of a New Rating Scale." *Archives of General Psychiatry* 51 (1994): 98–108.

Szara, S. I. "The Comparison of the Psychotic Effects of Tryptamine Derivatives with the Effects of Mescaline and LSD-25 in Self-experiments." In *Psychotropic Drugs*. Edited by W. Garattini and V. Ghetti. New York: Elsevier, 1957.

Vollenweider, F. X. "Evidence of a Cortical-subcortical Imbalance of Sensory Information Processing during Altered States of Consciousness Using Positron Emission Tomography and [18-F]fluorodeoxyglucose." In *50 Years of LSD: Current Status and Perspectives of Hallucinogens*. Edited by A. Pletscher and D. Ladewig, 67–86. New York: Parthenon, 1994.

13 LAW ENFORCEMENT AGAINST ENTHEOGENS

Is It Religious Persecution?

Eric E. Sterling

Eric E. Sterling, J.D., has served as president of the Criminal Justice Policy Foundation since 1989, working on issues of drug policy, violence prevention, sentencing, and the criminal justice system. From 1979 until 1989 he was counsel to the Committee on the Judiciary, U.S. House of Representatives, where he played a major role in developing anti-crime and anti-drug legislation and policy. In 1990, after *Employment Division v. Smith,* he worked with Reuben Snake in establishing the Washington office of the Native American Religious Freedom Project. He worked with the Native American Church of North America and the Coalition for the Free Exercise of Religion in passing the Religious Freedom Restoration Act of 1993 and the 1994 amendments to the American Indian Religious Freedom Act.

Our society is currently in the midst of a cultural-spiritual crisis. The decline of American civil religion—those traditional religious observances that combine Christianity with patriotism and social altruism—and the failure of orthodox religious practices to provide genuine experiences of transcendence have created a climate of spiritual deprivation and an intensified search for transcendental answers. Today, it seems, popular demand is for experience rather than theology or dogma, and for the direct inner knowing of mystical states.

While societal unrest and the disintegration of traditional institutions pose a serious threat to existing social structures, the popularity of spiritual groups offering a variety of pathways to transcendence calls for a new perspective on the part of observers attempting to formulate practical guidelines for healthy psychological and spiritual development throughout life. The challenge is to evaluate groups that claim to offer pathways to transcendence in terms that make sense to people who want to weigh the potential benefits of joining such groups against hazards of indoctrination, coercion, and authoritarian control.

FRANCES VAUGHAN, "HEALTH AND PATHOLOGY
IN NEW RELIGIOUS MOVEMENTS," 1987

SIT ON A quiet, sunny beach. Watch and listen to the waves rolling in. Watch and listen to the terns and gulls wheel and dive. Feel the sand blow up against your legs, gritty and rough. Here is peace and exquisite beauty. The wind blows across the dark water, moving the waves along. At points, a gust whips the water to foam, advancing the top of the wave. The top of the wave is blown off, and the wave is transformed. The addition of energy is profoundly transformative.

The movement of waves is one of the oldest forms of energy in human experience, but when additional forms of energy are applied, a person can see a wave in a new light.

Throughout existence, the judicious addition of energy has been transformative and has exposed God at work in creation, as the Great Designer of the interplay of the forces of life, as the Cosmic Choreographer. While everyone has the capacity to have direct experience of the divine, I don't think it comes easily, or the same way, for everyone. There are many techniques (or what we might fashionably call technologies) for adding energy, for inviting this experience, such as prayer, fasting, chanting, drumming, dance, or meditation—and these include the sacramental use of psilocybin mushrooms, LSD, peyote, or other entheogens. All of these practices can change a person's interior chemistry. The plants and chemicals that facilitate awareness of the presence of the divine are called "entheogens," from *entheos*, inspired, from *en* + *theos* (god). Some entheogens may be endogenous—produced or released within the body by prayer or by physical activity. Other entheogens may, when ingested, stimulate the release of internal psychic or spiritual energies that are usually held in check by habit or convention.

In a rundown neighborhood in an American city—in what used to be called a slum—gaunt girls solicit men. They offer a quick, meaningless, and dangerous sex act in exchange for a "rock." One cheap pleasure in exchange for another. Some of these girls have children—but they haven't seen their babies in hours or days or months. Nearby, boys with military weapons patrol the corner drug market or the armored crack houses where vials of crack are exchanged for cash. And the cash, collected in fives and tens and twenties, is gathered, bundled, shipped, trucked, flown, and eventually laundered, spreading out around the world in bribes and corruption. From the pathos of the streets and the brutality of the market to the peddling of influence, the buying of businesses and politicians, the greed becomes power—one of the great evil powers of our times.

Working to fight the greed and to protect the young—indeed

to protect the nation and the economy—policymakers and law enforcement officers are fully engaged in a "war on drugs." With these honorable motives, the agents of the DEA, the FBI, the BATF, the Customs Service, and local police struggle to enforce the law.

But the law, written and rewritten by office holders acutely sensitive to public fears, sweeps broadly, ever more broadly, to arm the police and to cover all "drugs," making little distinction among them. Thus the powerful compounds used for millennia to seek the divine, including peyote (whose active ingredient is mescaline) and psilocybin and their newer cousins LSD and MDMA, are banned.

Peyote, for example, was being used religiously by the Huichol people of north-central Mexico by the second century C.E. In 1620, the Spanish Inquisition denounced peyote as diabolic and made its use illegal. Mexican Indian peyotists were tortured and killed. By the 1880s, religious peyote use spread into North America but was subject to suppression by U.S. authorities and Christian missionaries. However, by the second decade of this century, the use of peyote was organized in the incorporation of the Native American Church. But even though some "sacred fireplaces" of the Native American Church adopted Jesus, the crucifix, the Bible, and other Christian elements, many Western states enacted laws against the use of peyote. Peyote was never used "recreationally" or as a "drug of abuse"; it was always used in religious practice. Peyote was classified by law enforcement authorities like a narcotic drug, not to stop its abuse, but to stop its religious use. However, because the federal authorities acknowledge the sovereignty of the Indian tribes and have a trustee relationship with them, the Bureau of Narcotics and Dangerous Drugs and later the Drug Enforcement Administration extended regulatory protection to Indian religious use of peyote. Still, many states continued to prosecute Indians, as well as non-Indians, for use, possession, or distribution of peyote.

In 1990, the U.S. Supreme Court, in *Employment Division v. Smith* (a case originating with the religious peyote use by members of the Native American Church), abandoned well-established standards of protection for the free exercise of religion and ruled that religious peyote use was no longer protected by the First Amendment to the U.S. Constitution. Religious leaders around the nation were shocked and, in response, created the Coalition for the Free Exercise of Religion. America's organized religions spoke with one voice in convincing Congress to renounce *Employment Division v. Smith* by overwhelmingly enacting the Religious Freedom Restoration Act of 1993 (PL 103–141). By enacting the American Indian Religious Freedom Act Amendments of 1994 (PL 103–344), Congress specifically remedied the Supreme Court's ruling in *Smith,* giving Native Americans (but only Native Americans) the right nationwide to use peyote in their spiritual practices. Congress recognized that use of peyote in ritual settings is not harmful.

Unfortunately for the rest of us, the Controlled Substances Act of 1970 (as amended by the Controlled Substance Analogue Enforcement Act of 1986, PL 99–570, sec. 1202) still broadly prohibits even the controlled use of entheogens for the most sacred and holy purposes. This is because the drug laws neither distinguish the entheogens from drugs like cocaine and heroin, nor their sacramental use from "recreational" drug taking. In their commitment to reducing drug abuse, lawmakers and the U.S. Drug Enforcement Administration and its allied agencies in federal, state, and local governments and around the world are tragically impeding the responsible religious practices of many gentle people and using against them the extreme measures developed to combat gangsters.

The world of gangsters, cartels, and mafias—and their law enforcement opponents—is a dark, dark world. It is a world filled with guns, secrets, and spies. Among the most valued persons in this world are those who can gather intelligence, those who have mastered the craft of espionage, the Mata Hari's, the seducers, those whose gift or expertise is to win the trust of suspicious people for the explicit purpose of betraying that trust. And of course it is easier to practice this "art" on those who are more trusting, such as those who are peaceful and spiritually inclined. Those who make, cultivate, or distribute entheogens have become the training targets for the heavy artillery of the "war on drugs."

Having seen the guns of the crack dealers, the skid rows where the junkies shuffle, and the hospitals where inconsolable babies cry, the men and women of the government forces and their allies are convinced that they are the "good guys" and it is their noble mission to "take out" the "bad guys." Empowered with broad statutes, regulations, and court orders, equipped with surveillance equipment, wiretaps, and techniques of coercion, the drug enforcement world brings these forces to bear not only on gangsters, but on people who produce, distribute, and use entheogens—the generally nontoxic and nonaddictive substances that, when properly employed, can open the way to the higher reality.

Many of our government agents were brought up in churches and synagogues on Main Street. They learned their Bible lessons. They have a faith, and they are comfortable living it. Many of them learned that religious tolerance is a fundamental American value. If someone else goes to a different church, or to a temple or a mosque and worships *their* God by another name, such as Allah, or with different words or prayers, they have a right to do so. But in practice, the extent of our religious tolerance is often very limited. In conceiving of and approving the First Amendment, the framers of our Constitution wanted to avoid the tragic wars of the seventeenth century in which one group of Christians warred against another group of Christians. But even with the First Amendment, religious-based violence has been frequent in the United States. Most Christians now recognize that it isn't right, after all, for Christians to threaten or force other Christians (or non-Christians, for that matter) to convert upon penalty of imprisonment or death.

Today, there is what some fear is—and others are proud to call—a "culture war," which advocates "preserving Judeo-Christian values."

The voices for toleration of differences are few, muted, or stifled. Every society wants to preserve the values of responsibility and care for others and of self-respect and care for self. But to foster responsibility and self-respect in entheogenic religious practices, the government's agents have not been content to merely teach or convince—as is the right of any citizen, and by the lights of many of their faiths, their duty. With the ever-growing authority of the law, the government and its agents use coercion against people, including Jews and Christians, who use entheogens in their religious practice. This may fairly be called persecution.

How can our society rule out particular paths to religious discovery and remain true to our most basic founding principles? Can our nation really be willing to revert to the seventeenth-century model of propagating "correct" beliefs through intimidation and actual violence?

Drug policies and enforcement efforts, as applied to entheogen users, are not much different from those of the Inquisition, which protected the "true faith" with the stake and other tools of torture from the danger posed by heretics and Protestants. Nor, as applied to entheogen users, are they much different from the measures used by Spanish *conquistadores* with swords and muskets to bring the "true church" to the native peoples of America.

If a group claimed that to worship its God it had to sacrifice a virgin and offer her heart to their deity, their claim of religious freedom would be denied, and the priests who so killed would be charged with murder. And no one would blame the law enforcement officers who investigated such a bloody cult. But where there is a good faith claim and tradition of spiritual seeking, where there is no harm, where there is no exploitation, then those who use entheogens have a legitimate claim to the protection of the First Amendment of our Constitution.

We teach our children that our national heritage of religious freedom was founded at Plymouth Rock when the Pilgrims waded ashore from the Atlantic's waves, free at last from religious persecution in

England. The term "enthusiasm" entered the English language in 1603 to characterize some dissenters from the established Church of England who held the then-controversial belief in special revelations of the Holy Spirit and religious fanaticism. Today it is equally controversial—and dangerous—to be a person, who was not born an American Indian, who uses those plants or chemicals to see into the essence of reality. Can't we learn from the spiritual teachings and practices of Native Americans, along with the more mundane agricultural and culinary lessons we remember on Thanksgiving day?

Those who use these plants and chemicals not only feel as persecuted as the Pilgrims or Quakers were in the seventeenth century, we are as persecuted in fact. "Enthusiasts" of the seventeenth century in England, such as the Quakers, were jailed by the thousands to stop them from worshipping. Those persecuted included William Penn, a Quaker held in solitary confinement in the Tower of London for a year, who founded Pennsylvania as a haven for religious liberty. The "entheogenists" of the twentieth century—without a haven—are being arrested by the thousands every year on drug charges, with no recognition of the religious nature of their activities. America must not allow this most un-American religious persecution to continue in the twenty-first century.

For law enforcement officers engaged in the protection of youth from the harmful effects of "drugs," it may be very difficult, given their training, to distinguish what appears to be harmful use of street drugs from the responsible use of entheogens in spiritual practices. But it is fundamentally the mission of the law to draw distinctions. Legislators who earn the most respect write laws that draw careful and appropriate distinctions between the permitted and the proscribed. The respect accorded lawyers and judges is, in part, recognition of their wisdom in hearing the evidence and making the judgments—oftentimes subtle—that maintain the full protection of the Constitution and its guarantees when they are warranted.

To enter the dark underworld of the drug trade requires bravery, which perhaps requires shutting oneself off from certain sensibilities. But it is our prayer that among those who have one foot in both worlds, there are some who recognize that our light is pure and has every right to shine, who will say so aloud. We pray that we can worship in peace and in safety in a corner of the world of light. And we pray that in our homes and gathering places we can use the extra help that entheogens can give to see into and through the foam of life and come to know the deep healing water of the sacred.

ABOUT THE COUNCIL ON SPIRITUAL PRACTICES

The Council on Spiritual Practices (CSP) is a collaboration among spiritual guides, experts in the behavioral and biomedical sciences, and scholars of religion dedicated to making direct experience of the sacred more available to more people. There is evidence that such encounters can have profound benefits for those who experience them, for their neighbors, and for the world.

CSP has a twofold mission: to identify and develop approaches to primary religious experience that can be used safely and effectively, and to help individuals and spiritual communities bring the insights, grace, and joy that arise from direct perception of the divine into their daily lives.

The Council on Spiritual Practices has no doctrine or liturgy of its own.

www.csp.org

CSP CODE OF ETHICS FOR SPIRITUAL GUIDES

[**Preamble**] People have long sought to enrich their lives and to awaken to their full natures through spiritual practices including prayer, meditation, mind-body disciplines, service, ritual, community liturgy, holy-

224

day and seasonal observances, and rites of passage. "Primary religious practices" are those intended, or especially likely, to bring about exceptional states of consciousness such as the direct experience of the divine, of cosmic unity, or of boundless awareness.

In any community, there are some who feel called to assist others along spiritual paths and who are known as ministers, rabbis, pastors, curanderas, shamans, priests, or other titles. We call such people "guides": those experienced in some practice, familiar with the terrain, and who act to facilitate the spiritual practices of others. A guide need not claim exclusive or definitive knowledge of the terrain.

Spiritual practices, and especially primary religious practices, carry risks. Therefore, when an individual chooses to practice with the assistance of a guide both take on special responsibilities. The Council on Spiritual Practices proposes the following Code of Ethics for those who serve as spiritual guides.

1. [**Intention**] Spiritual guides are to practice and serve in ways that cultivate awareness, empathy, and wisdom.

2. [**Serving Society**] Spiritual practices are to be designed and conducted in ways that respect the common good, with due regard for public safety, health, and order. Because the increased awareness gained from spiritual practices can catalyze desire for personal and social change, guides shall use special care to help direct the energies of those they serve, as well as their own, in responsible ways that reflect a loving regard for all life.

3. [**Serving Individuals**] Spiritual guides shall respect and seek to preserve the autonomy and dignity of each person. Participation in any primary religious practice must be voluntary and based on prior disclosure and consent given individually by each participant while in an ordinary state of consciousness. Disclosure shall include, at a minimum, discussion of any elements of the practice that could reasonably be seen as presenting physical or psychological risks. In particular, participants must be warned that

primary religious experience can be difficult and dramatically transformative.

Guides shall make reasonable preparations to protect each participant's health and safety during spiritual practices and in the periods of vulnerability that may follow. Limits on the behaviors of participants and facilitators are to be made clear and agreed upon in advance of any session. Appropriate customs of confidentiality are to be established and honored.

4. [**Competence**] Spiritual guides shall assist with only those practices for which they are qualified by personal experience and by training or education.

5. [**Integrity**] Spiritual guides shall strive to be aware of how their own belief systems, values, needs, and limitations affect their work. During primary religious practices, participants may be especially open to suggestion, manipulation, and exploitation; therefore, guides pledge to protect participants and not to allow anyone to use that vulnerability in ways that harm participants or others.

6. [**Quiet Presence**] To help safeguard against the harmful consequences of personal and organizational ambition, spiritual communities are usually better allowed to grow through attraction rather than active promotion.

7. [**Not for Profit**] Spiritual practices are to be conducted in the spirit of service. Spiritual guides shall strive to accommodate participants without regard to their ability to pay or make donations.

8. [**Tolerance**] Spiritual guides shall practice openness and respect toward people whose beliefs are in apparent contradiction to their own.

9. [**Peer Review**] Each guide shall seek the counsel of other guides to help ensure the wholesomeness of his or her practices and shall offer counsel when there is need.

The Code of Ethics for Spiritual Guides by the Council on Spiritual Practices, R. Jesse, convenor, is licensed under a Creative Commons Attribution-Share Alike 3.0 United States License. Copies and derivative works must contain a link to www.csp.org/code.

OTHER BOOKS IN
THE CSP ENTHEOGEN PROJECT SERIES

Cleansing the Doors of Perception: The Religious Significance of Entheogenic Plants and Chemicals
By Huston Smith

Psychoactive Sacramentals: Essays on Entheogens and Religion
Edited by Thomas B. Roberts

Religion and Psychoactive Sacraments: An Entheogen Chrestomathy
Edited by Thomas B. Roberts and Paula Jo Hruby
Published online at www.csp.org/chrestomathy

The Road to Eleusis: Unveiling the Secret of the Mysteries
Twentieth Anniversary Edition
By R. Gordon Wasson, Albert Hofmann, Carl A. P. Ruck

ISA AND THE DOUBTERS

It is related by the Master Jalaludin Rumi and others that one day Isa, the son of Miryam, was walking in the desert near Jerusalem with a number of people, in whom covetousness was still strong.

They begged Isa to tell them the Secret Name by which Isa restored the dead to living. He said: "If I tell you, you will abuse it."

They said: "We are ready and fitted for such knowledge; besides, it will reinforce our faith."

"You do not know what you ask," he said, but he told them the Word.

Soon afterward, these people were walking in a deserted place when they saw a heap of whitened bones. "Let us make a trial of the Word," they said to one another, and they did.

No sooner had the word been pronounced than the bones became clothed with flesh and retransformed into a ravening wild beast, which tore them to shreds.

Those endowed with reason will understand. Those with little reason can earn it through a study of this account.

The Isa in the story is Jesus, the son of Mary. It embodies a similar idea to that of the Sorcerer's Apprentice, and it also appears in Rumi's work again and again in oral dervish legends of Jesus, of which there are a great number.

Tradition invokes as one of its famous "repeaters" one of the first men ever to carry the title of Sufi: Jabir, son of el-Hayyan, the Latin Geber, who is also the founder of Christian alchemy. He died in about 790. He was originally a Sabean and, according to Western authors, made important chemical discoveries.

IDRIES SHAH, *TALES OF THE DERVISHES*

INDEX

229